PRAISE FOR *CIVIC PIONEERS*

"Fully relevant and significant to today's readers since many seem to long for a renewed sense of the power of public service . . . Very timely."

—Chad Berry, dean, Berea College

"The author was an accomplished leader in the public sector and very admired for her work in New York City. She walked the walk . . . I very much like what she tells us about herself, and other readers will like it too."

—Gerald Benjamin, SUNY New Paltz

"These stories powerfully illustrate the positive and long-lasting impact that service in the common good can have."

—Louise Mirrer, president and CEO,
New-York Historical Society

D08877989

CIVIC PIONEERS

Local Stories From A Changing America, 1895-1915

GRETCHEN
DYKSTRA

ISBN 13: 978-1-63489-208-7
LCCN: 2019934336
Printed in the United States of America
First Printing: 2019

23   22   21   20   19   5   4   3   2   1

Cover design by Rachel Adam
Interior design by Patrick Maloney

Wise Ink Creative Publishing replaces every tree used in printing their books by planting thousands of trees every year in reforestation programs. Learn more at wiseink.com.

For Bill Zinsser

How can we know who we are and where we are headed if we don't know where we have come from? How can we call ourselves patriots if we know little of our country's past?

—David McCullough

The happiest men I know in all this unhappy world of ours, are those leaders who, brave, loyal and sometimes in tears, are serving their fellow men.

—Lincoln Steffens

CONTENTS

INTRODUCTION

Benny's Hot Dog Stand, a funky, five-stool affair at the ratty southwest corner of 89th and Broadway on the Upper West Side of Manhattan, was an unlikely place to reawaken my interest in government. But that's where it started. In 1986, another breakfast club member—a fast-talking, whip-smart, politically savvy lawyer with a nervous tick—surprised me with a job offer.

He was the newly appointed executive director and counsel to the New York City Charter Revision Commission. Three women in Brooklyn had sued the city for violating the constitutional principle of one person, one vote. An archaic governmental body, unique to New York, decided budget and land use matters and approved contract and franchise deals, but its voting members did not represent the five boroughs fairly—little Staten Island had as much power as mighty Brooklyn. The case went all the way to the US Supreme Court.

The city had to remedy the problem. A commission made up of 15 volunteers with vast and varied experience in municipal government would review the city's constitution and present in a referendum to the voters the commission's recommendations for change.

My breakfast buddy asked if I'd direct the communications and outreach work and help get the referendum passed. I was working at a national foundation helping the recipients of its largesse communicate their agendas to policymakers, advocates, and other funders. It was fun, but far removed from the action. I knew a bit about politics, at least on the national level, but I knew little about local government. I certainly did not know that cities had charters, and I had no experience with the intricacies of municipal law and city services. I accepted his offer. No political science or public administration course could have taught me more.

The commission members met and debated—always in public—possible changes to the structure of the city's government and its land use, budget, and contracting procedures. Like a three-dimensional chess game, one proposed revision here would change things over there, and the advocates for "here" often hated the idea of "there." Sometimes our offices were open 24/7. Three years later, the referendum passed overwhelmingly and I was hooked on local government. I soon segued from inside city government to outside government on city issues.

In 1991, Times Square had become a mess, with petty criminals and filthy sidewalks defining the area. Strip joints, lap dancing, and multi-level porn shops set an edgy tone, appealing to some, threatening to many. Even New Year's Eve was losing TV viewers and the owner of the iconic ball was bankrupt. Theatergoers stayed away and hotel rooms and office towers stood dark and empty. As a result, property owners, led by the publisher of the *New York Times* and the Broadway theater owners, established a not-for-profit organization to make Times Square clean, safe, and friendly. They hired me to run it.

Supplementing city services and working closely with everyone from the mayor to cops and sanitation workers, we did everything from sweeping the sidewalks to saving New Year's Eve. The public-private partnership succeeded, and today Times Square is a clean, safe, friendly, and very crowded madhouse.

In 2002, Mayor Bloomberg appointed me commissioner of the Department of Consumer Affairs. Small business regulation and consumer advocacy became my focus. Bloomberg was a terrific boss, always following the rule of law, supporting his commissioners, and putting results ahead of politics. Then, as the first head of the National 9/11 Memorial Foundation, I tried hard, but unsuccessfully, to work within a dysfunctional structure, founded in pain. I quit before Mayor Bloomberg assumed control and brought order to the entire operation. I left the public arena.

But I did not lose my interest in local government. Memories of my grandfather led me back into municipal government, the world I knew best. Clarence Dykstra came of age when factories were displacing farmland, cities were growing rapidly, and massive immigration was rattling American traditions. From his hometown in Iowa, he gravitated to cities—Chicago, Cleveland, Cincinnati, Madison, and Los Angeles—going in and out of academia and local government. Respected nationally (he was even a clue in crossword puzzles), he was not, however, unique.

In fact, at the end of the 19th and beginning of the 20th century, the swift and radical technological, social, and economic changes across the United States enticed a wave of people to tackle new problems with new ideas. Active government began on the local level with people like Clarence Dykstra. Some addressed glaring inequality and injustice, others worked for political reform, and many, like Dykstra, professionalized public services. They were not ideologically monolithic. In fact, sometimes their agendas collided with other progressive agendas. But whatever their individual passions, they all believed government should and could advance society for the betterment of all.

I was curious about them. Who were they, what did they do, what motivated them? I went looking for them and found many. Here are some of their stories.

My criteria for selection were straightforward: Find interesting and compelling people who made a difference working for local government as industrialization, urbanization, and immigration radically transformed America. Tell their stories and see what traits they shared.

I profile thirteen people who were each responsible for a local or state agency between 1895 and 1915. Some were active long before those years, and others continued their work long after. All were well known in their day, and a few still are. Hollywood twisted the story of one, but most have been forgotten. Some identified as Progressives; a few were apolitical. Some were elected to their jobs; most were appointed. The final chapter, an outlier, highlights one issue rather than one person, as the major players were dramatic but not admirable!

Early on, I decided to search for people in different services. I began with Denis Swenie, the taciturn but courageous fire chief from Chicago; August Vollmer, the innovative postal-clerk-turned-police-chief from Berkeley, California; and George Waring, the flamboyant and effective sanitation commissioner from New York.

I wanted rural representation too. America was moving from the countryside to cities, but most people still lived rurally or in small towns. I found the fascinating but troubled Kate Barnard, one of the early settlers of Oklahoma, who devoted her formidable energy to defending Indian children. Charlie Mayo, the low-key, world-renowned surgeon, served as director of public health for his hometown of Rochester, Minnesota, pushing for pasteurized milk, one of the more interesting public health battles of the early 20th century and a bridge between rural and urban America.

In addition to regional diversity—10 different places are represented—I sought gender diversity. Highly principled, Katherine Bement Davis, Ella Flagg Young, and Frances Kellor had managerial might and impressive tenacity in prison reform, public education, and immigration rights, respectively. Two women from Chicago, Julia Lathrop and Lucy Flower, established the nation's first juvenile court, but as neither worked for government I coupled them with Judge Ben Lindsey from Denver, who spread the concept nationally.

Racial diversity was hardly a value embraced at that time, and government opportunities for minorities were sparse. But while focusing on public libraries, I came across Reverend Thomas Blue, who, inspired by Melvil Dewey and supported by Andrew Carnegie, creatively led two of the first "colored" libraries in the South. (I found no Latino, Asian-American, or Native American representation, but if I have overlooked someone, I would appreciate an introduction.)

If most of these civic pioneers have been lost to history, why should any of us care? Well, for starters, their lives make for good stories with glimpses into our shared past. We also drink clean water, feed our children pasteurized milk, enjoy safe sidewalks, and attend public schools in part because of these people.

But, more importantly, these people believed that we, the people, deserve clean water, public education, safe streets, a fair justice system, and honest government. In that respect, nothing has changed; the public still deserves those services and we often receive them.

Today it has become politically expedient to criticize, badger, and bully the very people who continue to work on our behalf. Ronald Reagan began this trend when he famously said, "The nine scariest words in the English language are 'I'm from government and I am here to help.'" That cynical joke is now repeated daily in appalling ways. But our daily lives depend on dedicated public servants. Maybe these stories from not so long ago will remind us of what we expect, what we deserve, and what can happen when committed leaders emerge to make the world a better place for everyone.

KATE BARNARD

Oklahoma's Good Angel
and Her Lonely Battle
for Indian Orphans

On November 16, 1907, the telegram from Washington, DC made it official. Oklahoma was a state.[1] Thirty thousand people—three times the number of residents in Guthrie, Oklahoma—gathered around that town's library. They rang bells, sounded sirens, and banged gongs; on the library steps, a white woman with some Cherokee blood "married" a white man, Mr. Oklahoma. Their fake wedding signified the formal unification of Oklahoma Territory with Indian Country. No marriage, real or symbolic, had ever begun in such loveless turmoil.

After the "wedding," the newly elected governor Charles Haskell, five congressmen, two future US senators, and every local dignitary rode a few blocks to the State House. Commissioner Kate Barnard, 33 years old and the only woman in the new government, rode alone in the last carriage.

Much later, she wrote in her unfinished memoir, ". . . a broken down, battered and frayed buggy . . . [its] lopsided top swayed dizzily, its back and sides shot through with holes. . . . I had always claimed to be a commoner, but, if I had any doubts about it, I was supplied with all the evidence and earmarks of it now."

Kate Barnard became the first woman ever elected to a major statewide office in America, winning more votes than any

---

1   Oklahoma was the 46th state.

other candidate including the newly elected governor—years before Oklahoma women could vote in the state or national elections.

Breaking every rule about proper deportment for women of the day, Kate Barnard boxed in the rough-and-tumble arena of politics in the tough West. She helped shape and pass the state's first constitution, and she had already done more and would do more for poor children in Oklahoma than anyone else. But she was not even listed in the official program that day, a harbinger of things to come. She later wrote,

"The Parade over, I fled from this perambulating skeleton to hide my embarrassment and ignominy in my office in the State House . . . Weary and exhausted, I climbed the long stairways to the third floor . . . I expected happiness . . . What I got was a hole in the wall, in the attic, hidden away under the projecting roof of the alcove behind the foul odors and flaming placard of the men's toilet."

Barnard, as Oklahoma's first Commissioner of Charities and Corrections, oversaw some 325 public and private institutions. She could go to court on behalf of individuals, but it was a position with little authority. She had no power to change the institutions. She could not hire or fire anyone. She could persuade people to change internally, or bring pressure on others for external change—a politically risky responsibility. She was paid less than her colleagues and had only a staff of three.

But she was a dogged fighter for the vulnerable in a raw society. Known as Oklahoma's Good Angel, Saint Kate, or just plain Kate, she made the state, for a brief moment, one of the most progressive in the union. "While men focused on streetcars, paving and skyscrapers, she fought for shorter hours, living wages and a more just relationship among men," wrote Joseph Thoburn, a well-respected Oklahoman historian.

But when Barnard exposed a broad conspiracy to rob Indian children of their land, she was stripped of power, her reputation was destroyed, and her physical and mental health were compromised. She died a broken woman.

A BRIEF DESCRIPTION OF OKLAHOMA'S COMPLICATED PAST

In 1803, the United States doubled in size with the addition of the Louisiana Purchase. A few Indian tribes—some sedentary, some nomadic—lived in what became Oklahoma. But in 1830, after years of political pressure from settlers in the east, President Andrew Jackson, with extraordinary paternalism and manipulation, signed the Indian Removal Act. The law gave him the legal power to "negotiate" the removal of Indians living east of the Mississippi River to twenty million acres of foreign land out west. President Jackson released a public statement, saying:

"Where you now are, you and my white children are too near to each other to live in harmony and peace . . . Beyond the great Mississippi River . . . your Father [meaning himself] has provided a country large enough for all of you . . . There your white brothers will not trouble you; they will have no claim to the land, and you can live upon it . . . as long as the grass grows or the waters run . . . ."

Over the next decades, Indian tribes from Arkansas, Illinois, Ohio, Wisconsin, and elsewhere were forced to relocate west. Five tribes (Cherokee, Choctaws, Creeks, Seminoles, and Chickasaw) from the southeastern part of the United States initially resisted militarily and politically, but most were forcibly moved. Trudging over rugged and unfamiliar land to their new "home," almost 25,000 of the 90,000 people died on that Trail of Tears. Known as the Five Civilized Tribes in deference to their absorption of Christianity into their spiritual traditions; their establishment of boarding schools, colleges, and courts; and their tribal structures, each tribe managed an elaborate set of treaties and legal arrangements with the federal government and its agents. But that experiment in autonomy did not last.

Those tribes, having practiced slavery in the South, sided with the Confederacy during the Civil War. When the war was over, the federal government retaliated and took away the western half of their new land for other Indian relocations and reservations.[2] However, between the western and eastern part of this vast territory lay two million acres of unassigned land. Unassigned, yes, unoccupied, no.

---

[2] Many of those slaves, as well as freed slaves, were forced on that infamous march, and Oklahoma still has some predominately African-American towns.

Texas ranchers grazed and drove their cattle through that land with impunity. The federal government did little to stop them, but would-be settlers who snuck into the area, repeatedly arrested and thrown out, saw the potential. They wanted the unassigned lands opened to them. Why should just a few well-financed ranchers get it all? After almost a decade of failed attempts, the settlers finally prevailed.

On April 22, 1889, some 50–75,000 people, including Kate Barnard's father, waited at designated spots along the border of these "unassigned lands." When bugles and cannons sounded at noon, they raced across the prairies in carriages, covered wagons, and buggies—some rode horses, some ran on foot, many hopped rail lines, hoping to beat the others. They raced to claim 160 acres somewhere in the vast expanse. It was the first of five "land runs."

White settlers arrived knowing nothing about Indian cultures and traditions. The Indian practice of communal property became most suspect. Many articles appeared about the strange habits of the Indians and their peculiar, downright un-American practice of joint ownership. After all, white Americans were, as the preeminent Indian historian Angie Debo wrote, "acquisitive and individualistic."

Consequently, the federal Dawes Act, enacted in 1893, just four years after the first land run, authorized the break-up of the remaining tribal lands. It took nineteen years to complete the task. Each deal differed, but heads of Indian households typically received 160 acres, unmarried adults 80 acres, and Indian minors 40 acres. The acres were rarely contiguous, making them less valuable to the Indian owner, and the price for any "surplus" land was as low as thirty cents an acre. The financial deals exploited the inexperience of the Indians in the private marketplace and legalized greed.

"Subject to the clamor of an irresistible white immigration and deserted by public sentiment, the situation of the Indians was hopeless," wrote Angie Debo in her book *And Still the Waters Run*.[3]

Often aided by corrupt lawyers, courts, and government officials, grafters, with the speed of vultures, swindled and robbed Indians

---

[3] The University of Oklahoma refused to publish her controversial book; Princeton did in 1940.

of their allotted timber, coal, oil, and farmlands. Indian children were their weakest prey. An estimated 100,000 Indian children in 40 counties of Indian Territory owned about $130 million worth of land and another $25 million in oil. The blatant theft of their land incensed and mobilized—and ultimately destroyed—Kate Barnard.

HER EARLY YEARS

Kate was born in the tiny farming town of Geneva, Nebraska, on May 23, 1875, to John Barnard, an Irish-American, and Rachel Mason, a young widow with two small sons. John was a restless entrepreneur. A lawyer, surveyor, real estate speculator, and railroad worker, he moved the family to a tiny town in Kansas where he bought two small lots of land. Before Kate turned two, Rachel died. Unable to cope alone, John Barnard sold the land, sent the three children to live with his in-laws, and went looking for work. Kate was shuffled among relatives for almost four years, never bonding with any of them.

"Winter is the only synonym for a motherless child's life," she later said.

Kate saw her father occasionally. When he remarried in Kensington, Kansas, he sent for her. Kate was six. But within a few months of the birth of a baby boy, John and his wife divorced.[4] This time John took Kate with him as he traveled from town to town. Her education was sporadic and her friendships few. In 1889, her father tried his luck in the first Oklahoma land run. Like most, he did not win the race that day, but he stayed in what would become Oklahoma City, the town that went from a population of zero to 10,000 in less than 24 hours.

Four years later, during another land run, John Barnard finally won a claim near Newalla, 25 miles southeast of Oklahoma City. Someone had to live there to legitimize the claim, so he sent Kate, now sixteen. She lived alone for two years in a two-room shack on the red clay land dotted with black jack oaks and hickory trees.[5]

---

[4] Divorce was rare in those days—3 or 4 percent.
[5] Her father visited regularly with supplies.

When she was eighteen, she moved back to Oklahoma City and attended Catholic school, earning a teaching certificate.

To modern sensibilities, John Barnard sounds irresponsible and unloving, but not to Kate. She revered him, and when he died in Texas when she was 34, she was devastated. "A stern man with a sense of justice . . . he never broke a promise. Justice to him was a passion," she wrote. He was a wanderer and she was a lonely child, but he imbued her with conviction and principles and maybe, subconsciously, anger at inattentive authorities.

KATE'S AWAKENING

In 1904, Kate Barnard, age 29, was a stenographer with the territorial legislature. She was chosen among hundreds of applicants to be the hostess of Oklahoma's territorial exhibit at the St. Louis World Fair. Poised and confident, with thick black hair that framed brilliant blue eyes, she was a perfect representative—attractive, comfortable with strangers, and a consummate networker.

The World's Fair, a kaleidoscope of popular culture and intellectual firepower, captivated Kate. With 1,500 exhibits, one on crime particularly intrigued her, as did lectures by Jane Addams and other social reformers. Spurred by what she heard, Barnard toured poor St. Louis neighborhoods. She saw the shanties and tenements of gritty industrial neighborhoods—Oklahoma's future if they were not careful.

Galvanized, Barnard offered her hometown newspaper a deal: Support me for two months in Chicago at the School of Civics and Philanthropy, and I will send you articles about what I see and learn. The editor agreed, and off she went. She visited Chicago's slums and studied theories of social and economic reform with professors at the University of Chicago. With her articles in the Oklahoma City newspaper, she raised awareness of what the future might hold and increased her public profile in the process.

She returned to Oklahoma City, ablaze with a cause. She resuscitated a local charity, raising money and soliciting contributions, and from her house she distributed food, clothes, and medicine to poor people. In two years, she assisted some 2,000 families. Her experience deepened her perspective and determined her future.

"What people need is not charity but justice and the chance to do an honest day's work for a fair wage. Charity is like pouring water into a sieve."

Contrary to convention (Oklahoma laws allowed women neither to vote nor to hold public office), she got involved with politics. Barnard ignored expectations and aligned herself with mine workers and progressive farmers in the Oklahoma Territory. It was simple: Fair wages for adults ensured good futures for children, and children were the future. Kate Barnard became an outspoken, highly visible, and effective advocate for them.

STATEHOOD AND ITS OPPORTUNITIES

The land runs onto "unassigned land" accelerated the clamor for representation in Washington, and for more than ten years contentious discussions ensued. Some people argued for statehood; some argued for a formal separation of Indians from Oklahomans; some suggested a state with a slow absorption of Indians as "they" became ready; the Indians just wanted their sovereignty. Soon white people outnumbered Native Americans six to one in the Indian Territory alone; statehood was inevitable.

Kate Barnard saw an opportunity. She went all in, working with other activists to shape the upcoming constitutional convention. A strong framework for the future state could take the best from other states and prevent the ravages of exploitation.

She spoke on steps and soapboxes, often facing protests, often inspiring people. She called for compulsory education and an end to child labor—an extremely unpopular notion among mining and railroad companies as well as farmers.

"If you farmers vote for child labor . . . I hope that . . . when the sap goes out of your cornstalks . . . that God will turn your cornstalks into the skeletons of little children and they will shake their dry bones at you," she implored the delegates at the Constitutional Convention.

She included in her list of demands the formation a Department of Charities and Corrections (and permission to a woman to run it.) Later Barnard was accused of self-interest, but the idea was not hers. It belonged to Hobart Huson, whom she met in St. Louis; he moved to Oklahoma City and became her deputy and loyal friend. Without this provision, Huson argued, Oklahoma, the state, would begin with no policies and practices to protect orphans, the insane, the jailed, and the disabled. Such a department was essential.[6]

OKLAHOMA'S ANGEL

"This little 96-pound bundle of nerves has frightened the politicians . . . because of her great influence with the union labor party," wrote the editor of the Guthrie newspaper after the election. Her colleagues respected, or feared, her electability, but they had little regard for her or her mission. Without any legal authority, Kate wielded no power to affect change.[7] None of that stopped her.

She moved on behalf of the forgotten with the speed of an arrow, and her well-publicized denunciations of inhumane conditions hit their marks over and over. In one two-week period, riding in horse-drawn carriages over unpaved roads, she inspected five jails, a school for the blind, an orphanage, and a sanatorium. With a flair for the dramatic, she wrapped herself in a sheet, entered a quarantined poorhouse, ordered immediate fumigation, and then blasted it as an "inferno," with residents "living like paupers in a five-cent hotel."

She discovered "paranoids, imbeciles, alcoholics and epileptics" housed together inside insane asylums. On a tour of a factory, she was horrified when a child looked up to smile at her and lost his

---

[6] Never married, Kate wrote about Huson, "I often marveled that such a man should remain single, but association with my secretive father taught me never to seek confidence where it is not volunteered." Indeed, Huson was married with two sons, and Barnard never knew it. When he disappeared from Oklahoma in 1918, their friendship was in tatters. He died penniless in the Salvation Army headquarters in New York with an unanswered letter from his sons in his pocket.

[7] As commissioner, she was paid $2,500 a year, but took $1,500, saying, "I cannot live on money that would rob little children of the necessities of life." One historian suggested that she took a lower salary to silence those who said she was self-dealing.

hand in a conveyor belt; she met children in factories breathing arsenic until they passed out.

"The vitality of these thin-chested, stoop-shouldered, sallow-cheeked, leaden-eyes, and pipe-stem figured children should not be expended in the morning of their lives . . . If we create degenerates by stunting the minds and bodies of little children, we cannot hope to have a strong and vigorous citizenship," she pleaded.

Oklahoma had local jails where children were often held with grown men, but it had no state prison. It shipped its convicts to Kansas and paid forty cents a day for their incarceration. Barnard traveled to Lansing, Kansas, to inspect the conditions there. She found cells the size of coffins; she saw a seventeen-year old boy hanging by irons in a dungeon for not digging his daily quota of coal. She heard about inmates thrown into deep holes and then covered in water. She learned that Kansas "contracted" inmates out to private companies.

After hearings and an explosive report, which infuriated the governor of Kansas, Oklahoma brought all 638 inmates home. Shackled to their seats, they shouted with joy as the trains began to move. Barnard won national fame with her action. The New York Times described her as an "eager, intense, fiery little person."

During her first term, she convinced the legislature to pass 23 laws including appropriations for a state prison, mandates to separate the sick and disabled from the insane, specific restrictions on child labor, compulsory education, and, unique in America, compensation for single mothers whose children were prohibited from working. Her progressive planks built a firm foundation for the future.

INDIAN CHILDREN AND THEIR STOLEN LAND

In 1908, the federal government gave Oklahoma judges the right to appoint guardians to "protect" Indian children from incompetent or unscrupulous parents selling their children's land. One year later, in response to a lead, Kate found three Cherokee orphans, with matted hair and empty eyes, living in the hollow of a dead tree, drinking from a stream, and begging for food from nearby farmers. Their court-appointed guardian had 51 other orphans under his "care." He collected royalties from the oil found on their respective lands and then "charged" the orphans for their "room and board." Soon Barnard identified 145 more Indian children whose land was being "managed" by guardians who declared the children "homeless orphans" and sent them to state institutions at the state's expense. Outraged, Barnard assumed the thefts extended way beyond orphanages.

Soon after her reelection in 1910, Barnard was given legal authority to supervise the affairs of all Indian children, not just orphans. She and her aggressive counsel, Dr. J. H. Stolper, discovered cruel and multifaceted scams: A county judge appointed guardians who struck deals with land developers to "use" the child's land; the guardian got a cut, the judge a kickback, and the child nothing. Sometimes the guardians forged deeds, and when the children turned eighteen, the guardians tricked them into "selling" their land at a fraction of its value. In the case of timberland, the guardians sold the harvest rights and kept the money, leaving the stripped land worthless. Several minors died mysteriously after they "bequeathed" their land to guardians. No laws required guardians to be accountable to anyone or any legal body.[8]

---

[8] The judges with the greatest number of Indians in their jurisdiction, although perhaps sympathetic, were overwhelmed, unable to conduct any thorough reviews of the guardianship applications or the long-term situations.

Word spread that Saint Kate cared. To identify cases, she and her lawyer relied on honest lawyers, concerned judges, Indian leaders, and sometimes children themselves. Here is one letter she received.

"Mr. Kate Beknard I will rite you a few linds to see what a bout my land the cort pointed Will J Brown a gardeen and I didn't no it . . . he had it for 50 dollars per year . . . the cort said if I could prove that he was not geten a nuff out of the land wood geve it Back to me . . . Lela Dixon, Weleetka, OK."

By the end of 1912, Kate Barnard and her counsel had taken 1,568 cases, won every single one, and regained more than $1.2 million for those children. Woefully underfunded and understaffed, however, Stolper focused only on surefire cases, disappointing concerned citizens and overloaded judges. Unfortunately, a boastful and arrogant man, he also treated adversaries, as well as potential allies, with a cold and dismissive tone.

Politically, his behavior hurt Kate, who had already made many of her own enemies. She often went public with her observations and her outrage, publicly chastising managers and their political champions of incompetence, cruelty, or both. After the legislative fight for limits on child labor, for instance, Barnard convinced the labor unions to denounce the speaker of the legislature, Alfalfa Bill Murray, who had not been sufficiently supportive of her efforts. A friend of the rich and the powerful and a blatant sexist (journalist John Gunther later described him as a "cantankerous hick in a burlesque show"), Murray despised Barnard from then on.[9] He got his revenge in 1913 when he and his colleagues stripped Kate's office of its meager funding, leaving money only for Kate and a stenographer—no other staff, no travel money, no telephone, no stamps. Barnard could hire another lawyer, the politicians said, only if she hired one of theirs.

She told a reporter, "There has come over [me] a loathing and disgust, a shrinking back from the sordidness, the venality, and the duplicity of politics."

---

[9] Undoubtedly a sign of his influence, a wooden carving of Alfalfa Bill Murray's wildly mustachioed face decorates the lobby of the grandest hotel in Oklahoma City, built in 1911.

Undeterred, however, Barnard traveled the state using private dollars, amplifying her accusations against the Oklahoma legislature, its congressional delegation, and federal officials. She attacked "hateful politicians who are destroying me politically because I will not give up the Indian work," declaring that $200 million more of vulnerable land was at stake. She lobbied to bring the federal government back into Oklahoma and, when it came, she accused it of political bias.

In November 1914, Cato Sells, the newly appointed federal Commissioner of Indian Affairs, after a fact-finding trip to Oklahoma, announced nationally, in an extraordinary response to an article by Barnard, that she was correct. Corrupt lawyers and courts had robbed Oklahoma Indians, including 100,000 children, of millions of dollars of land. He announced that federal lawyers would supervise some 30,000 outstanding cases. Commissioner Sells urged the state to approve a package of laws that included a fixed fee for guardians and open bids for oil and gas lands. Oklahoma did so.

Kate Barnard might have felt vindicated, but it was too late for her. Tired, sick, and broken, at age 39, she retired and virtually disappeared.

KATE BARNARD'S SAD AND LONELY END

She had been sickly for several years with respiratory, cardiac, and nervous conditions, and had often traveled out of state to visit doctors, giving Oklahoma politicians more ammunition against her. One summer she had even checked into the New York State Neurological Institute to seek a cure for her "hysterical pain."

With no relationship with her half-brothers and few, if any, friends, Kate Barnard returned to the lonely status she knew as a child. She lived off money she inherited from her frugal father and rental income from the land in Newalla, and she fled to "the wilds of Colorado mountains." She worked briefly as a counselor for Judge Ben Lindsey, her hero in juvenile justice reform, but that did not last long. She was sometimes spotted wandering aimlessly, maybe slightly unhinged—sometimes asking strangers if she could weed their gardens.

She returned to Oklahoma City, where her health worsened.

Every three weeks or so, excruciating red lesions with white, pus-filled blisters erupted on her face and neck, sometimes in her nose and throat. Desperate to ease the pain and humiliation, she sought cures from multiple doctors, pharmacists, chemists, and dentists around the nation; her diary contains twelve pages of their names and affiliations. Baffled, they diagnosed everything from gallbladder problems to cancer to germs. She soaked in Lysol baths, dabbed Epsom salts on the lesions, took quinine, modified her diet, mixed herbs, swallowed arsenic, and once even allowed a dentist to drill a hole in her lower lip to release the "parasites." It is possible that she suffered an extreme case of coxsackievirus, which was not identified until 1948.

She lived at the Egbert Hotel on busy North Broadway with a restaurant on the ground floor and a medical building next door. Progressively more reclusive, she spent time writing her memoirs on 315 tiny pieces of paper. She entitled one section "The Leaders Who Shaped Human Destiny in Oklahoma from 1905–1914 and What Became of Them."

Rightfully and poignantly, she included herself: "defeated, disillusioned, her office wrecked, her Life's Work destroyed . . . ostracized, isolated, hated, damned . . . and forgotten . . . drifting sick and alone . . . struggling desperately to regain her health and rebuild her shattered life."

She typed continuously late at night. When other residents complained, Kate Barnard was moved to the top floor, away from others. She died there, of a heart attack, in her bathtub on February 23, 1930. She was 54 years old.

She wanted her land in Newalla to become the Oklahoma Home for the Friendless, but her estranged half-brother and two stepbrothers contested her will and won. She was buried next to her father in Oklahoma City; the state only recently placed a full-size bronze statue of her on a bench in a far corner of the first floor of the State Capitol. Few people know who she is, or read the plaque, when they sit next to the statue for photographs.

DENIS J. SWENIE,
Chief of the Chicago Fire Department.

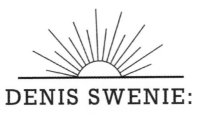

DENIS SWENIE:

Chicago's Courageous Fire Chief

George Francis Train, an independent candidate for president of the United States, was a handsome egomaniac with a flair for the theatrical. On the night of October 7, 1871, wearing his signature white vest and lavender kid gloves, he told a large audience in downtown Chicago that "a terrible calamity is impending on the City of Chicago . . . More I cannot say, more I dare not utter." The next day, Chicago burned to the ground in an epic catastrophe. Some asked if he started the fire.

But that infamous Great Fire of 1871 did not change much in government. The fire department remained tiny, the politicians denied it resources, its chief still had no authority, and no one enforced the few building codes. Change only came three years later, after another fire, dubbed the "little big fire," prompted national underwriters of insurance policies to pull out of Chicago in frustration. Finally, the city leaders listened, and Denis Swenie, the modest firefighter with a gruff demeanor and a courageous record, made the Chicago fire department world-class.

BRED-IN-THE-BONE FIREFIGHTER

In 1837, little Denis Swenie climbed undetected over a makeshift gate and wandered down a dirt road to find a bonfire some big boys had set in his hometown of Glasgow, Scotland. Clapping and laughing, the three-year-old was a happy boy when his mother found him. At five, he disappeared again to watch firefighters at a burning warehouse; by ten, he was chasing, and often riding on, carriages rushing to fires. The firefighters all knew his name; both his father and uncle were volunteer firefighters in Glasgow. His obsession was bred in the bone.

Glasgow in the mid-1800s was a sizeable city with a university and royal hospital, but the cattle and sheep markets and their ancillary industries of weaving and dyeing provided most of the jobs to the city's poor residents, including Denis's family. He was born there on July 29, 1834, one of five children, to Irish Catholic parents. Swenie used to say that it was the Irish in him that got him into fiery patches and the Scotch in him that kept him there. The family immigrated to the States when Denis was twelve, arriving in Chicago in 1848.

There, he worked in a shop making fire hoses and joined the nearest volunteer fire brigade, running with lanterns in front of the horse-drawn carriages. Then he became the "hose boy," responsible for keeping the hoses dry and rot-free; soon, when fires raged, he was dragging hoses to the river or later to a water main, if allowed, and over time to fire hydrants. He mastered "throwing" water that rushed from the hose at 500–800 gallons per minute.

Back drafts, explosions, buckling walls, collapsed floors, blinding smoke, and scorching flames were constants in Denis's life—and, in brutal Chicago winters with icy water and freezing winds, he faced it all, gloveless, in a rubber coat with icicles dripping from his hat. He survived concussions, broken limbs, cracked ribs, burned hands, a scorched back, and seared hair. He suffered the loss of many people. It takes a steady temperament and supreme confidence to fight fires, in addition to courage and selflessness, and Swenie, in a gruff way, had both. Denis Swenie became chief in 1879, and stayed in that position until 1901. He became a Chicago institution.

BEFORE THE GREAT FIRE, A DYNAMIC TINDERBOX

Incorporated in 1833 with 150 people, a few houses, and one tavern, by 1870 Chicago was home to more than 340,000 people. The "gem of the prairies" was booming. Second only to New York in energy, it bustled with commercial life along the Chicago River and Lake Michigan. Railroads, docks, lumber mills, grain elevators, slaughterhouses, and stockyards defined Chicago in those early days, and wood shaped it.

Half of the city's 93,000 buildings were wood. Easy to use, the wood was brought south on wooden trains or in wooden boats from the dense white pine forests that covered the upper Midwest. Massive piles of timber lined lumber mills, and woodworking shops were knee deep in shavings, sawdust, and wood chips. Wooden grain elevators, served by steam engines often fueled by wood, towered over the densely packed neighborhoods of jerrybuilt, one-story wooden houses. Sheds full of hay, wooden corncribs, and wooden pigsties often stood out back. Many fashionable mansions and commercial buildings were wood-framed, sometimes covered by flammable brick. Wooden shelves and wooden floors made up the downtown stores. People used kerosene lamps to light their spaces and wood in stoves to heat them in winter. More than 550 miles of wooden sidewalks, raised from 3 to 10 feet, wound through the city's four quadrants. A veritable tinderbox, Chicago averaged two fires a day. That first tavern, opened in 1833, burned down in 1851.

FIREFIGHTERS AND INSURANCE PATROLS

Chicago knew it was vulnerable. Right from its beginning, tin stovepipes and leather fire buckets—one for each stove—were required. But Chicago, like most cities and towns, depended on volunteer fire companies, and an unpaid chief, elected annually, "managed" the volunteers. Few chiefs had any firefighting experience, and most served just one or two years before losing the next election. The volunteer companies with names like the Red Jackets, the Fire Kings, and the Forty Thieves often brawled at fires, fighting for the honor, oysters, beer, or money that came from appreciative victims.

In the mid-1800s, Chicago suffered a fire that started when a prostitute kicked over a lantern in a brothel. The firefighters had spent the day before at a county fair, competing to see how far they could "throw" water; consequently, the hoses were in bad shape.

Twenty-three people died, including ten firefighters. Volunteer Denis Swenie, age 23, found 18 of the 23 bodies in the rubble.

After that fire, angry businesses and insurance companies established insurance patrols with paid employees. When the patrols, often housed close to firehouses, heard an alarm, they rushed to the fire, trying to beat the volunteers so as to save valuables and prevent looting by unscrupulous volunteers. In 1858, the City of Chicago, tired of the ensuing chaos, hired its first paid firefighters. They worked alongside volunteers and tensions mounted. Denis Swenie became the first paid chief engineer and faced his own opposition when he introduced a steam engine into the department—another change the volunteers resented.

THE GREAT FIRE OF 1871

The summer of 1871 was hell. A severe drought and high temperatures ravaged the Midwest and, by the end of September, Chicago was fighting 25 fires a week—four on October 5, five on October 6, and a particularly destructive one on Saturday, October 7, the night of George Train's prophetic lecture. That fire started in a lumber mill and burned well into Sunday afternoon, destroying many blocks and a firehouse. All 216 firefighters, both paid and unpaid, were exhausted, and several fire trucks were out of commission. The night that Mrs. O'Leary's cow purportedly kicked over a lantern in the barn behind her house in the southwestern part of town, human error and inadequate equipment fueled the flames.

At first the firefighters were sent in the wrong direction; by the time they arrived, fifteen fires were burning in Mrs. O'Leary's neighborhood. The winds had kicked up and fires were spreading north and east toward downtown. Alarms rang throughout the city. The bell on the courthouse pealed continually until fire destroyed the building and the bell toppled into the street below.

Embers—called red snow—fell through open windows onto people asleep in their beds. Burning shingles flew onto rooftops, starting new fires. Fire devils, columns of cyclonic air that form when the heat of a fire meets the cool of the air, hurled flames from one burning building to another. One fire devil hit the steeple of a church that sat between a furniture factory and a woodworking mill. Ferocious flames erupted. Efforts to block the fire with dynamite failed, and water from hoses evaporated before it hit the flames. Perhaps most lethal, the elevated wooden sidewalks became "horizontal chimneys," with flames shooting under them, spreading the fire throughout the southern part of the city and into the central business district. Wooden boats burned on the grease-slicked Chicago River and a kerosene tanker exploded, lighting up the river in horrifying color. Pigeons were sucked into the flames and cattle and horses stampeded. By 3:30 a.m., the pumping station was gone.

One little girl screamed in agony as fire scorched her, and a quick but foolish man doused her with liquor, thinking that would extinguish the flames. Mary Lincoln and her son, living at the Tremont Hotel, escaped before it was destroyed and ran to Lake Michigan where many people waded deep into the water with their backs burned and their lungs roasted. Other people ran west into the prairies, some hid in tunnels, and a few huddled in empty graves. They were the lucky ones—300 people died in that fire.

The firefighters, including Denis Swenie, then a captain of the Gund Engine Company, chased the fires for 48 hours as the flames incinerated the city and people panicked. Though the flames blew Swenie off his feet, he remained tough and determined. He climbed onto a rooftop alone to break a hole in it and let fire and smoke escape. He crawled under an engine through thick smoke to free its hose and, on his hands and knees, led a blinded steam engine driver to safety. He brooked no foolishness and hosed drunks who impeded his work. Many years later, people were still talking and writing about "the most remarkable cool nerve and judgment ever shown in a fire."

Two days later, rain finally arrived and the fires died down. They had burned a path four miles long and three-quarters of a mile wide, destroying houses, churches, the telegraph company, hotels, factories, offices, lumber mills, bridges, boats, a major newspaper, and the telegraph company. Seventy-five thousand people were left homeless, an estimated 18,000 buildings destroyed, and one third

The Bigelow Ruins, 1871

of the city's entire value was gone—an extraordinary $185 million. Only half of that was insured.

In the immediate aftermath, the city was quiet, but soon rumors of looting and murder spread unease. Inmates had been released from the burning jail, which fed a press frenzy in the following days. Martial law was established, but, much to the consternation of the public, the guards protected only the ruins of banks and other wealthy properties, doing little to organize relief operations. Martial law soon ceased. In November, Joseph Medill was elected mayor on the Fireproof Ticket. A well-respected editor of the Chicago Tribune, he only served two years before stepping down for health reasons, but in that time, he tightened Chicago's finances and began reconstruction.

The hot-button issue was who could build what where. The city established a new district for lumber industries, but proposals to extend citywide prohibitions on wooden houses were fiercely contested, seen as blatantly unjust to most people. The price of brick had escalated from $6 to $17 for 1,000 bricks, and few could afford them. Thousands of people marched against city hall in January 1872, and the city relented: All wooden structures that survived the fire could remain, and people who had lost a house could rebuild a temporary wooden structure if they replaced it within one year. That provision was not enforced, however.

Financial calamity followed the flames. Chicago had an estimated 200 insurance companies, most underwritten by national firms. With such stiff competition, local agents kept their premiums low. Unable to pay claims after the fire, 68 of those 200 insurance companies went out of business, and only 40 percent of the owners of insured buildings ever received any compensation.

THE LITTLE BIG FIRE

Fires continued in Chicago—smaller, of course, and often contained within one building, one factory, or one house, but, in mid-July 1874, a large fire started in a wooden barn next to an oil factory in a poor part of town that had been spared before. The fire destroyed some 800 buildings where many immigrants and African Americans lived and prostitutes worked. The fire stopped only when it reached a firewall, built after 1871 to protect the new buildings of the central business district. Chicago's "little big fire" claimed far fewer lives (20) and far less property damage ($3 million) than the Great Fire of 1871, but, once again, it underscored how poorly prepared the city was.

The National Board of Underwriters, the group that guaranteed insurance payouts, was incensed. From its headquarters in New York, the board hammered Chicago officials about their notorious political meddling in the fire department, the number of vulnerable buildings, and the numerous commercial hazards. Receiving no satisfactory response from Chicago's elected officials, the underwriters pulled their support, and forty insurance companies stopped covering buildings and businesses in Chicago.

The city leaders finally paid attention. They strengthened the code and extended the fire limits, established building permits, required fire escapes in some buildings, implemented new inspection regulations, purchased new equipment for the fire department, enlarged water mains, and gave the fire chief authority over a newly restructured fire department.

THE CHIEF

Resisting political machines and insisting on meritocracies was a hallmark of the new breed of leaders. Chief Swenie, with his brusque demeanor and consistent values, was a prime example, engendering respect in both mayors and his men. He never sent firefighters to fires he himself would not fight. In fact, his wife and the mother of his six children, Martha, once said, without a hint of regret, "Since the day we stood up in the little church together, he has regulated his life and mine, too, by the clanging of the bell."

Examples of his steadfastness abound, but one is particularly telling. In August 1894, the fire department responded to 1,226 alarms, including a "million-dollar fire" that began in a lumber area. Swenie fought the fire with his men, returning home at 3:00 a.m. He fell into bed fully clothed, but within thirty minutes an explosion right behind his own house woke him; he quickly ran to that fire. As he was fighting it, he heard that the first fire had reignited and threatened to spread into an entire district of the city. Swenie left the fire behind his house and rushed in his horse and carriage back to that fire, telling the crew to save his wife but not to worry about his house.

If a fireman broke the rules—with, say, too much drink—he dreaded facing the chief, as transgressions often led to dismissal. Sometimes a firefighter in trouble would send his own mother, wife, or sister to Martha to plead his case. Although Swenie rarely accepted excuses or granted leniency, Martha, with broad shoulders, a kind heart, and no fear of her husband, might intervene. She became a "real mother to every man in a great department."

Although Martha might get Swenie to change his mind, he never changed his style for the politicians or the powerful. He refused to hire, promote, or otherwise bend the rules for someone's cousin or friend. He was known to throw the presumptuous out of his office with explosive anger—this in a city known for its ward politics. Multiple mayors "lacked the nerve to touch him," wrote Jon Teaford, the urban historian. Swenie took pride in promoting from within, recognizing talent, and enhancing morale. A model chief in a model department, "He established the merit system long before it was even discussed by anybody, and it was from this system that such good came to the department," Mayor Carter Harrison said.

New firefighting technologies demanded new skills, and the increased size of the city demanded new men. During his tenure, Chief Swenie hired more than 1,000 new firefighters and won budget increases for improvements in the firehouses and the installation

of new alarm systems. He trained the men on all the new technologies and equipment, from hook-and-ladder companies to batter-
ing rams to fireboats. Property damage from fires plummeted from
$4,548 in the 1860s to $551 by 1885.

THE CHICAGO WORLD'S FAIR AND SWENIE'S FURY

By 1890, Chicago had buried its fiery ruins and emerged triumphant. It was back and bigger than ever—even if filthier—with
first-rate cultural institutions, diversified businesses, strong universities, and powerful industrialists; it had even boldly annexed sub-
urbs to increase its size and population. Its visionary architects and
builders were building taller and taller buildings more and more
quickly downtown. Consequently, debates about height, materials,
and fireproofing were a constant, and, although Swenie garnered
respect and trust, he continually had to argue for the importance
of fire safety.

When the US Congress chose Chicago over New York to host
the coveted 400th anniversary celebration of Columbus's discov-
ery of the New World, Chicago saw its chance to make a grand
entrance onto the international stage. Even Paris took note of
Chicago's global ambitions, warning that the upstart city could
never compete with Paris's spectacular world's fair of 1889.

Those were fighting words for the competitive Daniel Burnham,
the genius behind the fair's master plan and construction. Burnham
and his high-powered colleagues from around the nation designed
and built in less than three years 630 acres of parkland, including
the first-ever midway and 200 temporary buildings—all designed
in a cohesive classical style. Determined to set a new standard for
city beautification, Burnham had little time, or patience, for fire
prevention.

Chief Swenie insisted that the fairgrounds have six firehouses
and an entire battalion of firefighters. Burnham balked, arguing
that was far too expensive for only a six-month run.

"This committee is so cheap it wouldn't buy a spider for a blind
fly," snapped Swenie.

But Swenie, always willing to push back against authority or, in this case, Burnham's stature, prevailed, and the fair ultimately had scores of fire alarms, a fireboat on the manmade lagoons and lakes, and auxiliary firefighters recruited and trained to work alongside the regulars.

The fair opened to great acclaim on May 1, 1893. Laurence Gerckens, an urban historian, believes that the success of the exposition was fundamental in shaping 20th-century American cities. But six weeks after the opening, a small fire broke out in the five-story building that housed a massive "refrigerator" for perishables and an indoor ice skating rink.

Burnham had not liked an iron smokestack that protruded from the roof, breaking the aesthetic flow. He demanded that it be hidden. The contractor had done so. Although the fire was quickly extinguished, Chief Swenie called the building a firetrap, and told the organizers to fix it, predicting more trouble if they did not. On July 10, 1893, it happened.

With 30,000 people watching from below, another fire broke out at the top of the unprotected smokestack. Firefighters climbed into the central tower that rose high above the roof to reach the smokestack. But embers fell through the open space around the smokestack, spreading the fire onto the roof below the firefighters, engulfing them. Fifteen people, including twelve firefighters, perished.

The next day, a furious Swenie and his colleagues listened as Burnham and others denied cutting corners or ignoring warnings just to save money and protect aesthetics. One of Swenie's deputies would have pummeled the building's managers if the chief had not restrained him. As it was, one of the deputies was accused of negligence. Although a grand jury refused to indict him, the wound to the department and Swenie was deep and painful.

A SHORT RETIREMENT

On January 1, 1901, after fighting fires for more than 50 years, Chief Swenie retired at age 67. He had started as a volunteer with a leather bucket and ended as the most respected chief in the nation. He professionalized and depoliticized the department, making the city far safer and doing it with integrity and courage. Retirement did not suit him, however. His health failed him, and he died on February 16, 1903.

At his funeral, a colleague said, "If Swenie ever gloried in his reputation as a firefighter or felt a glow of pride over achievements that made his name throughout the entire continent, he kept the feelings to himself."

One year later, Lincoln Steffens published *The Shame of the Cities*, his blistering attack on the corrupt politics of American cities. In it, he cited Denis Swenie as the exception that proved his point—apathetic voters allowed corruption to fester. Swenie probably would have ignored the compliment, too busy fighting fires and advocating for better fire prevention.

Col. Geo. Haring

COLONEL GEORGE WARING

and the Victorious Street Sweepers of New York

The Great Hall at Cooper Union in New York City was built for grand civic affairs, and the memorial service for Colonel George Waring was certainly that. Almost 900 people squeezed into the wooden pews that November day in 1898. As they waited for the service to begin, 500 boys, some no taller than a broom handle, marched through the back doors, carrying banners, singing songs, and bringing the audience to its feet with wild clapping. The Juvenile Sanitation Leagues had come to pay their respects to the most famous garbage man in America.

Colonel Waring was not the first person who tried to clean up New York, but he was the first to succeed. He cleaned the streets and forever raised the bar of expectations in the city and beyond. Colonel Waring led the first modern and effective sanitation department—arguably the most essential and, if done right, the most invisible of all city services.

THE POLITICAL AND PHYSICAL DIRT OF NEW YORK CITY

The filth of New York was deep, foul, and legendary, and had been ever since the Dutch first settled the southern tip of Manhattan. In 1800, 60,000 people lived in Manhattan; 90 years later, one million lived there, making it the largest city in the nation.

As more and more people occupied more and more of the island, the garbage piled up: trash, ash, food, and the excrement of dogs,

cats, pigs, and goats. People threw their private garbage and emp-
tied their privies onto streets and into empty lots. Slaughterhouses
and butcher shops turned the streets red with blood. Animals
roamed freely, rummaging through heaps of garbage, adding their
own waste to it, and sometimes dying on the streets, their carcasses
feeding the flies and maggots.

In many ways, the horses were the worst. Approximately
150,000 toiled daily in Manhattan, each leaving about 30–50
pounds of manure a day, in stables and on streets, much of it
caught in the creases of the cobblestones, much of it never cleaned
up. At 46th Street and the East River, one notorious pile of horse-
shit, 30 feet high and 200 feet long, sat in an empty lot and poi-
soned the air for 30 blocks.

Wealthy women held perfumed handkerchiefs to their noses
and parasols over the heads to avoid the ubiquitous mess coming
from windows and the distasteful stench coming from everywhere.
Guttersnipes and street urchins picked through the garbage for
things to sell; some said the waste of the wealthy was the death of
the poor. "The filthy rich left the poor filthy," writes one historian.

When yellow fever and cholera struck, as they did periodical-
ly, they brought vomit, diarrhea, pain, and death to their victims.
Only those who could leave the city were safe; no one else was im-
mune, and the poor suffered the most. One medical study in 1863
estimated that 60–70 percent of all residents of densely populated,
dark tenements were sick at any one time.

Such epidemics, thought to be caused by the filth and the stench,
often spurred good intentions. Health workers cleaned and disin-
fected neighborhoods, apartments, tenements, and streets, but the
tidiness never lasted long. Corrupt city government—and in New
York it was the notorious political machine of Tammany Hall—
continually cut the thread of change.

The corrupt leaders gained and maintained their power and
built their fortunes by controlling every level of municipal government. They provided work in return for votes, not caring if the
tasks were done well; they gave contracts in return for kickbacks,

the more the better; and they made official appointments in return for acquiescence. Their influence stretched from the sidewalks to the courtrooms.

In 1881, under pressure from civic activists appalled by the filth and concerned for the well-being of the people, the city established a Bureau of Street Cleaning, centralizing the function instead of dividing it among police and health workers as it had been done in the past. But Tammany Hall was still very much in control.

Unsupervised and underpaid day laborers working as street cleaners were important for the votes they cast, not for the garbage they collected. Private carting companies had city contracts through the money they paid out of sight, not for the standards of their work. Judges served at the pleasure of the machine and ignored cases brought against well-connected transgressors like the notorious stable owner on 46th Street.[1]

In 1894, a determined and cagey minister, intent on awakening his rich and influential congregation to the ills of Tammany Hall, went underground to expose the corruption of the police force and its connection to the machine. Dressed as a country bumpkin, he visited dives where girls danced naked, children drank beer, and men solicited sex. He returned to his pulpit to tell the sordid tales, which gave rise to a well-publicized inquiry that revealed the interconnectedness of vice, police, and Tammany Hall. The inquiry galvanized the voters, who threw the bums out—temporarily—and opened a window of opportunity when a reform mayor, William Strong, was elected.

The mayor asked Theodore Roosevelt to take the job at the Department of Street Cleaning, but he rejected the offer, wanting instead to be police commissioner. Then a formidable group of upper-middle-class women, undeterred by all the previous failed efforts to clean the city, lobbied the mayor to hire Colonel George E. Waring. It was a smart and inventive choice.

---

[1] It took six years to get the stable owner punished and the infamous horse manure removed.

When Mayor Strong approached Waring, who had seen the last commissioner consistently blocked by Tammany Hall, Waring said, "I get my own way."

"The law gives you that to a large extent," the mayor replied.

"I do not mean the law; I mean you. You can remove me, but you must not interfere with me."

Strong never did, and although at times he might have regretted his promise, Waring, through strict discipline, strategic planning, effective management, and a commitment to public engagement, made history and cleaned up the filth.

EARLY YEARS AND A GROWING NETWORK

George Waring was born in 1833 in Pound Ridge, New York, a small agricultural community about forty miles north of New York. He attended the long-since defunct Collegiate School in Poughkeepsie, New York, where his father manufactured stoves. He then studied informally under a distinguished chemist, Dr. James Mapes, whose interests included ways to increase productivity on farms with chemical fertilizers, crop rotation, and tree conservation. Waring took to these new, scientific ways to farm.

Meanwhile Horace Greeley, the hugely influential and iconoclastic editor of the *New York Tribune*, bought 78 acres of land north of the city in the tiny hamlet of Chappaqua, New York——not far from Pound Ridge. Greeley's wife liked the land for its running brook and thick evergreens. Greeley fancied himself a model farmer, writing a regular column in the Tribune entitled "What I Know about Farming"—or what some real farmers referred to as "What I Do Not Know about Farming." Greeley soon discovered the inferiority of his new land as periodic floods and the perennial swampland made it difficult to cultivate the land. A perfect place to experiment.

He occasionally attended a private club in New York that brought chemists and farmers together, and it was probably there where he met James Mapes. Although Greeley never used Mapes's newly patented fertilizer on his weekend farm—he preferred printers' ink—in 1855 Greeley hired young George Waring, presumably recommended by Mapes, to solve his drainage problems.

"All lands . . . in which the spaces between the particles of soil are filled with water within less than four feet from the surface (except during and immediately after heavy rains) needs draining," Waring explained in one of the many books and articles he published later in his career.

Knowing Horace Greeley set Waring on his way. With definite opinions, freely offered, and a powerful bully pulpit, Greeley had deep connections in a national network of social reformers, including the young, footloose journalist Frederick Law Olmsted. Both abolitionists, Greeley and Olmsted once sent a howitzer to anti-slavery settlers in Kansas. They also shared an interest in experimental farming.

Olmsted's wealthy father bought his son a farm on Staten Island, hoping to focus his creative son's ambitions, but the younger Olmsted had trouble making it profitable. Like Greeley, Olmsted hired Waring to drain his property. Waring successfully solved the drainage problem in what he described as a "malarial breeding ground." Some think he might have rented Olmsted's farm for a while.

DRAINING CENTRAL PARK

About 1,600 pig farmers, gardeners, and black Americans lived in shantytowns in swamps punctured by granite outcroppings in the middle of Manhattan. Their presence made planning a park there a contentious and long, drawn-out process. But in 1857, Frederick Law Olmsted and Calvert Vaux, a British landscape architect, won the prized contract to design and construct Central Park. It was Olmsted's first design. But none of their plans for the lavishly designed terraces, pastoral meadows, planted promenades, transverse roads, and hilly rambles could happen before the massive wetlands were drained. They turned to 24-year-old George Waring.

In June 1858, Waring mobilized 400 workers to implement a plan developed in England. He supervised the work from atop Vixen, an old mare he bought from a peddler who traveled back and forth along the Hudson River selling clams and potatoes. Waring gave up smoking cigars to pay for the horse.

"Her most satisfactory trait was her fondness for her master," Waring wrote in a beguiling collection of horse essays, published in 1875, that softened the hard edges this tough and pragmatic realist exhibited.

In only six months, the workers dug (by hand) four-foot-deep ditches in parallel lines forty feet apart throughout most of the park and laid sixty miles of clay pipe to drain the immense swamp. It was the largest drainage project in America. They exposed natural streams, buried others, filled a lake in time for winter ice-skating, and made possible the wonder we see today.

This high-profile project and Waring's growing awareness of public health issues then steered him toward sanitation, but first the Civil War intervened. In that horror, Waring solidified his managerial skills.

MILITARY SERVICE AND LESSONS LEARNED

In 1861, Waring and Vixen marched to war with the Union Army, eventually winning a coveted place in General Fremont's cavalry in Jefferson City, Missouri. Sadly, Vixen, kicked by "an infernal brute of a troop horse" and then weakened by a virus, died before Waring faced his first battle.

"She rubbed her nose against my arm and was evidently thankful for my caresses, but showed no disposition to rise . . . and then she gave me a little neigh of farewell . . ." He buried her under a great oak tree.

Promoted to colonel—a title he would use for the rest of his life—Waring, now commander of the Fourth Missouri Cavalry, rode south to Mississippi in 1864. After a cold and rainy winter with muddy skirmishes along the way in thick forests, Colonel Waring and his men joined 8,500 other Union soldiers to confront General Nathan Forrest and his 4,500 soldiers at Brice's Crossroads outside

Tupelo, Mississippi. Waring's cavalry dismounted and fought hand to hand.

The Union Army ultimately retreated, losing twice as many men as the Confederates, but they succeeded in their mission: General Forrest never stopped General Sherman. Waring's performance sealed his reputation, and he would apply the lessons he learned, instituting a paramilitary structure at the Bureau of Street Cleaning, demanding discipline, and stressing merit over special favor—something unheard of in those days of messy and corrupt city governments.

OGDEN FARM AND MEMPHIS

Waring enjoyed hobnobbing with rich people. Upon his return from the war, he accepted a job managing Ogden Farm, an experimental farm in Newport, Rhode Island, an enclave of the hugely wealthy. From this perch, Waring introduced Jersey cattle to America and developed and sold the Trophy tomato, a new variety whose taste could survive shipping.

Waring traveled to Europe, where he discovered the new field of sanitation engineering, a field rich with potential for the public and his own future fortunes. He patented one of the innovations he saw in England: a system to separate rainwater from sewage, as opposed to combining them. Many civil engineers believed that combined systems were as efficient and more cost-effective than the separate system, if conditions warranted it.

When Waring left Ogden Farm entirely in 1877, he stayed in Newport, where he established a lucrative consulting company, advising the rich on their individual estates, consulting with cities and towns on their sewage and sanitation problems. He promoted the separate system he'd seen in England, which he dubbed the Waring system. Many saw this as an unethical appropriation of someone else's idea and a conflict with clients. Consequently, Waring was never invited to join the prestigious American Society of Civil Engineers.

He also wrote extensively about sewers for technical people as well as a general audience—a somewhat delicate topic for mainstream readers. He believed, as many others did, that stagnant water, rancid drains, and "sewer gases" were the cause of most communicable diseases. This miasma theory became gospel, even among medical doctors, who were slow to adopt the evolving, modern views of bacteriology.

Colonel Waring "proved" his theories in Memphis, Tennessee. When cholera and two yellow fever epidemics hit there, all within several years, half the residents of the city left and half of those who stayed died, an estimated 10,000 people. It shocked the nation; in response, the newly established National Board of Health hired Colonel Waring as their advisor He said quarantine was insufficient; entire new sanitation systems were needed.

Memphis hired him, and, beginning in January 1880, he and his crews worked quickly to clean the streets, lay 24 miles of pipe, fill outhouses, replace private privies with water closets, connect houses to sewers, clean cisterns, disinfect some houses, demolish others, and ventilate many. The miraculous changes in Memphis spurred great enthusiasm in many cities. One commentator said, "The sewers of Memphis solved the sewage of Paris."

WARING, THE MANAGER, AND HIS CROWNING GLORY

Colonel Waring began his job as commissioner of the New York City Department of Street Cleaning on January 15, 1895. Some thought he was nuts to take such an impossible and distasteful job; others thought it was beneath him. But within one month,

9 Varick Street
before Waring

a massive winter storm hit the city, dumping four feet of snow on the streets. Waring immediately lobbied the mayor for more resources to remove all the snow; in the past, only key boulevards were cleared. He argued that if all the streets were not shoveled, poor people would not leave their densely populated, under-heated rooms, and disease would spread. Waring released his letter to the mayor to the public too—a gutsy if impolitic move, boxing in the mayor. It worked. The mayor granted him the emergency resources.

". . . sometimes I have been a sore trial to him [the mayor] . . . and he has wished he might wash his hands of me . . . but he saw reasons for bearing with me until the storms blew over," Waring wrote later.

Waring quickly employed supplemental day laborers whom he paid promptly, deployed his own workers to clear the gutters and the crosswalks, and negotiated a new arrangement with the street-car companies to clear their tracks of the snow. In just one month, Waring spent $180,000 on the one snow storm, compared to the $59,000 his predecessor had spent for the entire previous winter, and with that money, Waring and his crews cleared almost seven times more snow.

Tammany Hall and its newspaper, the tabloid of the day, immediately began criticizing Waring, which they continued to do throughout his three-year tenure. They said he was profligate, wasting taxpayers' money. They predicted property taxes would rise to support his initiatives. But the clearing of the snow got people's respectful attention. Waring passed his first test with high marks.

If snow was his inauguration, his workforce was his second chapter. In the past, street cleaners were hired because of who they knew and they lost their jobs because of who they did not know—they had neither job security nor incentives to do a good job. That had to change. Waring assured the men that no matter how they got their positions, he would not fire them if they did their jobs. He started by firing lazy and incompetent supervisors and replacing them with former military colleagues.

Like other innovative leaders of the time, Waring believed that government could improve people's lives, but not if government was inefficient. He was a first-rate manager. For the first time, the department became a meritocracy with firm and uniform discipline, just like the army. Work hard, treat the public well, make the department proud, and do not drink. Those were his orders. "A good Colonel makes a good regiment," he immodestly wrote.

"What has really been done is to put a man instead of a voter at the other end of the broom handle," he wrote in his book *Street Cleaning*, published by Doubleday in 1897 and a direct challenge to the power of the political machine.

Using data to solve problems was another hallmark of these days. Waring assessed each street—what was done there, how busy it was, and its location relative to other activities. He evaluated each street and deployed his men accordingly. Waring assigned 15 to 35 men (40 percent of his workforce) to individual sections with a supervising foreman who reported to a district supervisor who reported to a deputy commissioner.

For the first time, neighborhoods like Five Points, known for its densely populated tenements, poor immigrants, and dirty streets, were cleaned alongside Fifth Avenue with its elegant stores and imposing mansions. The street cleaners swept 283.5 miles of city streets twice a day and 35.5 miles of busy commercial strips four times a day. Waring collected the data.

He assessed their equipment—its appropriateness, weight, usefulness, and cost. He made sure every sweeper had a two-wheeled cart, a broom, a scraper, jute bags, and a shovel; in the summer, they carried watering cans and hydrant keys so they could dampen any dust their sweeping produced. They worked an eight-hour day, every day; another 600 men in horse-drawn carts picked up residential and commercial garbage and ash, and then collected the jute bags left by the sweepers on the curbsides. The system was hierarchical, orderly, common-sensible, and revolutionary.

But change does not come easily. Waring publicly quarreled with the comptroller over whether subcontractors had to follow civil service rules. He won that fight by threatening to pull the sweepers off the streets. Without men to take the garbage to sea, what's the point of picking up garbage from the sidewalks, he said. The comptroller relented.

His most problematic relationships were with the workers themselves, at least initially. Within a month of his arrival, labor demands began, although there were no municipal unions yet. The workers wanted extra money for Sunday work, they were angry that a one-day absence would result in a two-day docking, and they insisted that Waring stop hiring "new" Italian immigrants as day laborers for snow removal, rubbish sorting, and shoveling from the scows. (The Italian head of the drivers' association made that demand.) Waring said no and threatened to cut their $2 per day pay to $1.50 (which he did not do).

Tough but not inflexible, however, Waring established a mediation process, spurred by the Women's Municipal League. Some thought it was a ruse: "Look out for Waring—this is one of his tricks." Thirty-five representatives from the sweepers and the drivers and nine from the stables met three times a month (without forfeiting any pay) to review individual grievances and refer some to a senior committee to settle. The department listed fifty offenses it would enforce, including unexcused absences, galloping horses, and failure to pick up stones from the streets. In its first year, the workers' committee heard 345 cases and sent 124 to the board, which included five members of the workers' committee. The workers' grievances included claims of brutality by foremen, late wages, and unfair docking. The system worked.

GOVERNMENT AS INNOVATOR

But the garbage itself was Waring's greatest challenge and the source of his most creative innovation: recycling. Before he had arrived, contract workers would pick up wet garbage that made it to the centralized dumps and then load it onto scows and transport it to sea where they threw it overboard, pretty much anywhere they wanted, not following rules of proper distance from shore. It invariably washed onto the shores of New Jersey and the outer reaches of Brooklyn, infuriating people there. Furthermore, the city also dumped ash and wet garbage on the then–87 acre Rikers Island, sending a stench across the East River to Manhattan.

Colonel Waring released a formal request for proposals for the disposal of garbage and signaled that the contract would no longer go willy-nilly to a buddy of Tammany Hall. Special interests no longer ruled. He reviewed some twenty responses on the basis of technical issues, experience, and cost and chose one, based solely on competence and price. Next, he ordered that ordinary rubbish be tied in bundles, a sensible and inventive regulation. Tammany Hall called him Miss Sissy Waring.

Imagining he could raise revenues from the refuse, he extracted grease and fertilizer from wet garbage and sold them to soap factories and southern cotton plantations. He sorted rubbish for potential resale; the first picking yard was at 18th Street at the East River. Rubbish that had no resale value was incinerated (Waring envisioned producing electricity from the burn) or mixed with ash and used again as landfill at Rikers, but this time without the stench. His ingenuity kept rolling.

WARING AS SHOWMAN

Good communications are necessary to awaken and maintain public support and, subsequently, political support. Waring understood this and excelled at public relations. He dressed the street sweepers in bright-white uniforms with white pith helmets—white like doctors and helmets like soldiers. The medium became the message. The uniforms also made it easy for supervisors to spot the workers! The street sweepers became known as the White Wings, sometimes fondly as the White Angels.

Initially ridiculed, the street sweepers did not like the uniforms or the money they had to spend to buy them. But their attitude changed in May 1896 when Waring inaugurated the first annual parade of street sweepers in the city. People, sometimes seven to eight deep, lined Fifth Avenue to watch and cheer as the flamboyant

Colonel Waring and his hundreds of public servants marched. Waring, dressed in his military outfit, topped with a white pith helmet like his men, sat ramrod straight atop a handsome brown filly and led 1,400 sweepers in their white uniforms with brooms over their shoulders from 59th to 26th Street. A thousand other employees in freshly painted carts pulled by well-groomed horses, ten marching bands, and mounted police followed them. Sanitation workers became city heroes, their work now seen as essential and life changing.

Waring had to look no further than the Lower East Side for another promotion with a purpose. The University Settlement House, the first such organization in the nation, was a neighborhood hub for poor immigrants living in squalid conditions in derelict tenements. Unable to speak English and most illiterate, they were relegated to work as street peddlers or sweatshop workers if they were lucky, at saloons and whorehouses if they weren't. The University Settlement House provided social and recreational activities, lectures, and lessons, helping them adjust to the realities and complexities of a new nation. It opened the first kindergarten, managed public baths, offered literature and history classes, taught English, and offered activities for young people to keep them out of danger and inculcate in them civic pride and individual responsibility. Its Juvenile Sanitation League, an afterschool club, taught young boys about, and encouraged them to take responsibility for, cleanliness in their homes and neighborhoods. Waring heard about the league, saw its citywide potential, and multiplied it 44 times.

"To arouse civic pride . . . is not distinctly within the province of the Department of Street Cleaning . . . and to use the influence of the children is not a new idea, but one practically untried," he wrote. By the end of his tenure, the Juvenile Sanitation Leagues, usually sponsored by local organizations, enrolled more than 1,000 young people, primarily in poor neighborhoods. They became cheerleaders for cleanliness. With club constitutions and officers, badges, certificates, songs, and field trips, they pledged to be part of the solution, not the problem. They learned about waste streams

and landfills and educated their parents, often non–English speak-
ing immigrants, and their friends about the importance of cleanliness. They became the eyes and ears of the department, sending
it weekly reports on conditions on their blocks. Waring received
letters like this:

"Dear Colonel Waring, I saw a man eating a banana. He took the
skin and threw it on the sidewalk and I said to him, 'Please, Sir, will
you be so kind and pick it up' and he said, 'All right . . .'"

HIS FINAL CHAPTER

Colonel Waring left city service when Tammany Hall returned to
power in 1898. That October, after the end of the Spanish-American
War, President McKinley sent Waring to Cuba to advise the federal
government on yellow fever prevention. He found despicable conditions in Havana and quickly devised a comprehensive $10 mil-
lion plan: Do not rely on quarantine, build sewers, pave the streets,
drain the malarial marshes, reorganize and fund the department,
and build an incinerator.

Tragically, Colonel Waring contracted the fever and returned
to New York very sick. Scared the public would panic, the head
of the Board of Health, ironically, ordered Colonel Waring to be
quarantined at home. Four days after his return, he died of yellow
fever. His corpse was placed in a hermetically sealed metal coffin,
taken on a "quarantine tugboat" to Swinburne Island in New York
Harbor where he was cremated. No formal funeral was held, only
memorial services at St. George Episcopal Church and eventually
one at Cooper Union.

The federal government implemented his plan for Havana, but
Waring died still believing that bad smells caused disease. Soon the
proponents of germ theory prevailed and, by eradicating mosquitoes, they eliminated yellow fever from Cuba; Major Walter Reed
led that effort. Medical advancements in bacteriology did not di-
minish Colonel Waring's contributions, however.

"His broom saved more lives than a squad of doctors. And it did
more; it swept the cobwebs out of our civic brain and conscience,"

said Jacob Riis, the chronicler of poverty in New York. A poor woman in a tenement had only three photographs in her room: the Virgin Mary, St. Joseph and Colonel Waring. When asked if she prayed to Waring, she answered, "No, my children and I thank him."

Although Tammany Hall shut down Waring's mediation process and eliminated the white uniforms and the Juvenile Sanitation Leagues, Waring's was not a passing triumph. Tammany Hall replaced Waring with one of his own, who maintained the paramilitary structure, and the resources kept flowing. In fact, City and State magazine wrote after Waring's death:

"His career furnishes the refutation to the charge constantly and flippantly made among us that a reformer cannot be practical." Indeed.

FRANCES KELLOR:

The Stalwart Champion of Immigrants

In 1908, Frances Kellor and Lillian Wald invited Governor Charles Hughes to dinner at the Henry Street Settlement House on the grimy, congested Lower East Side of New York. Wald, a public health nurse, had established the vibrant community center to help poor immigrants adjust to America. That year alone, 1.2 million people poured into New York; one third of them stayed in the city, squeezed together in decrepit tenements. Kellor directed a social science research organization with an interest in employment. As one historian writes, Kellor "dragged Wald into the depths of men's filthy industrial sites."

The federal government had recently established the Dillingham Commission to address the challenges of the "new immigrants." Inspired by that initiative and stirred by Kellor and Wald's impassioned advocacy and convincing facts, Governor Hughes soon appointed the first-ever state commission on immigration to "make a full inquiry . . . into the conditions, welfare and industrial opportunities of aliens in New York State." Unlike the Dillingham Commission that had nine members, all men and all elected officials, Hughes appointed Kellor and Wald, social activists and women, to his nine-person board.

The commission held hearings, heard testimony, and conducted research, but Kellor and Wald wanted to see the conditions for themselves, so they went traveling. Two others joined them: Mary

Dreier, Frances Kellor's lifelong partner[1] and the wealthy daughter of a successful German businessman who volunteered her time and talent organizing women in the workplace; and Lewis Hine, the schoolteacher-turned-photographer famous for his shots of small children working in factories and immigrants on Ellis Island.

The four drove 1,250 miles over unpaved, rutted roads, often in rain, carrying their own gasoline, visiting worksites and camp-sites. New York State and New York City were spending millions of dollars to extend the Erie Canal and construct the second fifty-mile aqueduct to New York City, betting, correctly, that these two massive projects would drive the future prosperity of the state. The workers felled trees, dug ditches, constructed dykes, built dams, and slept and ate in nearby camps. Most of the workers were newly arrived Italians, Poles, Austrians, Russians, and Hungarians—the "new" immigrants.

Although the construction contracts detailed the scope of the work, the materials, and the machines required, the contracts for the employees' livelihoods were vague. The housing contractors, called padrones, earned a flat fee per man per day (approximately five cents) to supply each worker with room and board. But with no minimum standards set, the more the padrones scrimped on the workers, the more money they made.

The four travelers visited 21 camps, ranging in population from 14 to 2,000 men, and "found huge locks, deep cuts, daring feats of construction . . . and barracks and shacks of the most primitive and humanly wasteful types." They saw windowless, wooden barracks with dirt floors and terrible odors where 100 men shared 65 bunks; they saw stagnant pools of filthy water and ate minimal and revolting meals. At one camp that allowed families, 100 small children hung around with no school to attend. Saloons and "rear rooms" in jerrybuilt shacks dotted the periphery of some camps, which hustlers and hookers invaded each payday.

---

[1] Kellor and Dreier had what was known as a Boston marriage, a lifelong emotional and interdependent relationship. They lived together, Dreier supported Kellor financially, and they shared common interests and commitments.

In 1909, the New York State Commission released its report, enriched by Kellor and Wald's observations and Hines's photographs from the field. The report reviewed immigrants' work and how they found work, if they found it; their housing and the "missionaries" who helped them; and schools or the lack thereof, transportation, common scams, courts, and private banks.

Once immigrants entered the country, only a few needed special protection, but most needed some assistance, the report stated. The lucky ones had relatives or friends or found their way to settlement houses, immigrant aid societies, or religious organizations.

"They have availed themselves of the opportunities here with remarkable avidity, contributing in return to the prosperity and intellectual development of this country," the report said. But the "methods by which aliens may become valuable citizens have been generally ignored."

With 80 percent of immigrants unable to speak English and the overwhelming majority past school age, the assimilation challenges both the state and the immigrants faced were massive. Immigrants had to learn about American values and expectations on their own. The report recommended establishing a Bureau of Industries and Immigration to address these challenges. In 1910, Frances Kellor became director of that office, the first woman to lead a New York State bureau and the first agency of its kind in the nation.

HER EARLY YEARS

She was born Alice Frances Kellar (she later changed the spelling of her last name) in Columbus, Ohio, on October 20, 1873, but moved immediately to Coldwater, Michigan, a county seat on the railroad line between Chicago and Detroit. No one knows why she and her mother moved there, and nothing is known about her father. She had a much older sister and some whispered that Alice was her illegitimate daughter, but that was never proven.

Her mother was a simple, hardworking domestic worker for families in town. She and Alice, purported to be one of the poorest families, lived in a rented room not far from the high school. Alice attended school for a while and was known as the best student there, but she dropped out to help her mother. She dressed like a boy, shingled her hair like a boy, and used a slingshot like a boy. Any disapproval of her appearance and her tomboy antics was offset by the respect she garnered from most adults in town who acknowledged her spunk and intelligence. Indeed, as her career flourished, she returned regularly to Coldwater to visit her mother, who died in 1919. The town celebrated her accomplishments.

Cool and confident, Alice enjoyed the company of adults and became a regular at the local "Ladies' Library," whose intellectually alive librarian, Mary Eddy, encouraged Alice to attend discussions, debates, and lectures on topics as challenging as eugenics and immigration—both of which engaged Alice later in life. For a while, Alice lived with Mary and her sister, Frances. Their active engagement with ideas impressed her, as did the sermons and friendship with Reverend Henry Collins, the minister of the Presbyterian Church. A graduate of Yale and Union Theological Seminary, Reverend Collins sparked Alice's social consciousness.

At age 21, after several years of working for the local newspaper, Alice accepted the financial help of the Eddy sisters and went to Cornell University, where Reverend Collins's brother taught and where one did not need a high school diploma for entrance, just the successful passage of ten entrance examinations. One of 83 female students, she studied law and graduated with honors in 1897.

She had not much liked the study of law, but was challenged by contemporary problems. Alice, who, by that time, used her middle name, Frances, as her given name and, for unknown reasons, now spelled her last name with an "o", enrolled as a graduate student in sociology at the University of Chicago.

Opened in 1892, the university made its mark quickly on the landscape of higher education and social reform. John D. Rockefeller endowed it and Marshall Field donated the land. Its president, William Raney Harper, who had received his PhD in classics from Yale at age eighteen, articulated a compelling vision: "The times are asking not merely for men to harness electricity and sound, but for men to guide us in complex economic and social duties."

Distinctly different from its Eastern counterparts, the University of Chicago admitted both men and women, sought students from around the world, combined the best of English and German universities, and actively sought a role in shaping the city. Promising a community of scholars interested in cracking the rigid silos of the classic academy, it drew some of the nation's best professors to its six stone buildings on a muddy prairie and encouraged interdisciplinary learning—a unique and radical notion.

Kellor reveled in the university's emphasis on the collection of data to understand and then solve real-life problems—an ivory tower with a firmly grounded foundation. She lived at Hull House, reinforcing her admiration for social reformers—in this case, the famous Jane Addams.

As her main research topic, Kellor explored and ultimately challenged eugenics, the widely accepted theory that intellect and character are inherited. This invidious notion of biological inferiority led to harsh restrictions on immigrants deemed unfit, an unduly harsh and unforgiving criminal justice system, discrimination in employment, and even forced sterilization. With energy and resolve, this tall, auburn-haired young woman traveled more than 3,000 miles alone through eight Southern states, comparing the physical attributes and environmental realities of white and black college women with more than 300 incarcerated African American women. FAK, as she now signed her papers, crafted comprehensive questions and data collection methods and looked at the most granular details, including how many women chewed tobacco, how many used snuff, how many swore, and how many were sexually active.

Aiming to be "an unprejudiced expert," FAK compiled her findings and wrote articles and, in 1901, a book: *Experimental Sociology*. The book challenged two well-known criminologists who argued that prostitution was hereditary, and with it Kellor garnered the respect of other scholars and researchers. (Thomas C. Leonard, a

contemporary economist at Princeton, recently analyzed the work
of scores of scholars, educators, and even preachers who in the early
20th century actively advocated for eugenics and race science and
built entire systems around those theories. Leonard does not men-
tion Frances Kellor.)

In 1902, Frances Kellor moved to New York.

NEW YORK IN 1902

The second massive wave of immigration to America had begun,
and the numbers were staggering. Ellis Island, once a hanging
ground for pirates, now served as the gateway to America. The first
immigrant through the process in 1892 was Irish, but her shipmates
were mostly Russian Jews, fleeing an oppressive regime and herald-
ing a dramatic change in immigration patterns.

The "old immigrants" who had first come in great numbers
to America were British, German, Irish, and Scandinavian. They
came primarily for economic reasons and, except for some Irish
and German Catholics, most were Protestant and fair-skinned. But
these "new" immigrants were primarily from southern and eastern
Europe, escaping political and religious persecution as well as poverty. They were mostly dark-skinned, unaccustomed to democratic
ways, culturally alien, and not Protestant.

America had changed too. Lumber, coal, iron ore, and oil were
fueling the rapid industrialization of the country. In the last three
decades of the 19th century, their production numbers swelled
by 9,000 percent! Patents for technological innovations increased
by some 2,000 percent and industrial jobs followed; the railroad
crossed America and a transatlantic cable was laid.

Although one third of all Americans still lived in towns smaller
than 2,500 people, many more Americans were leaving farms for
cities than the other way around. Their rural customs and sensibilities were challenged by new jobs, new filth, new diseases, and new
heterogeneity.

This new world not only urbanized America, but it also produced
colossal, untaxed wealth for the few who controlled businesses and,

in turn, the political realities of America. Many lived in grandiose, gilded mansions, flaunting their worth, separated from the people who worked in their mills and fired their ovens.

Henry George, the political theorist, describes this Gilded Age as an "aura of gold over dull metal," as thousands upon thousands of people, both old and new immigrants and native-born Americans, lived deeply insecure lives. Plagued by periodic unemployment, low wages, bad working conditions, terrible living conditions, and the constant fear of more mechanization, the working class became progressively more desperate and demanding.

In the late 19th century, some 37,000 strikes paralyzed cities, plants, mills, and mines. People were killed, private militias were established, and cities like New York and Chicago built massive armories to accommodate the National Guard when they were re-called to quell political and labor unrest.

Between 1901 and 1910, Ellis Island processed eight million peo-ple, a whopping 21 percent increase in the US population, adding greatly to the already existing tensions in the country.

Anti-immigrant sentiment was not new in America. Benjamin Franklin questioned why Pennsylvania "should become a colo-ny of aliens." The Know-Nothing Party of the mid-1800s made anti-Catholicism their rallying cry, suggesting that a papal conspiracy was plotting to take over America. In 1882, the federal government stopped all Chinese immigration. And making immigration even more difficult and complex, it was often the "old" immigrants who persecuted or exploited the "new" immigrants of the same heritage.

Immigrants were blamed for every American ill: rampant al-coholism, infectious diseases, job losses, crime, violence, political upheaval, societal unrest, and corrupt government. Some of these sentiments were pure racism, but some were based on sad facts: Immigrants often ended up in poor houses and hospitals in large numbers and in saloons drunk, and, as labor turmoil grew, some immigrants did protest or instigate strikes.

No one whispered their prejudices behind closed doors, and, given advancements in printing presses and postal systems, such thoughts spread quickly and widely in books, magazines, newspapers, and pamphlets. Cartoons were particularly cruel: They portrayed poor immigrants as apes eating off American plates or as anarchists carrying knives and dynamite. Uncle Sam was depicted holding his nose as bent and ragged immigrants begged to enter the gates of America. This was the climate in which Frances Kellor, age 36, shaped the Bureau of Industries and Immigration, using government's power to help the immigrants and help America.

FACTS AND ACTION AT THE BUREAU OF INDUSTRIES AND IMMIGRATION

The federal government managed Ellis Island and determined who could enter America, enforcing restrictions against "idiots, imbeciles and feeble-minded, people with contagious diseases, professional beggars, unaccompanied minors, disabled people, bigamists, anarchists, and prostitutes."[2] But federal jurisdiction ended as soon as immigrants disembarked on the docks of lower Manhattan. Then they were on their own.

At the bureau, Kellor began with a simple and profound philosophy: Society benefits when it helps immigrants adjust and find productive work, and immigrants assimilate more readily and completely if America treats them fairly and equally, encouraging their independence and their civic involvement. The initial definition of Americanization, later warped, was about self-sufficiency, understanding, and loyalty, not coercion or change.

"Immigrants, who have lived the narrow static domestic life of peasants, on arrival are homeless, unemployed, migratory . . . and unattached . . . once admitted the immigrant faces conditions, such as no American-born resident [has faced], and the state should recognize and meet [it] squarely," Kellor wrote.

The existing, uncoordinated network of charitable, fraternal, and religious organizations, like settlement houses, was important,

---

[2] Passengers who traveled first or- second-class on the ships did not have to go through Ellis Island. By dint of their ticket price, they were deemed acceptable and went straight to the docks.

but not sufficient—not by a long shot—and, in some places outside New York City, no benevolent organizations existed at all.

Kellor began with the immigrants themselves. She could not learn from immigrants and then help immigrants if they did not know the bureau was there. So she placed announcements in 962 foreign language newspapers all around the nation, saying, "The State wants to know what the difficulties and problems of its law-abiding immigrants are, why they fail and where they succeed, and to make them, if possible, helpful to the next stranger that comes in."

As such, the bureau served as a funnel, gathering information from immigrants and its own investigators, looking for patterns of abuse and then pursuing administrative or legal responses. The bureau had subpoena powers, but only five bilingual investigators for the entire state. One inspector was Carola Woerishoffer, a wealthy Bryn Mawr College graduate who had bailed out all the women arrested after the shirtwaist strike in 1909 to the tune of $75,000. Fearless, she drove herself around the state, inspecting camps, but in September 1911, at age 26, she was killed when her car skidded off an embankment.

In spite of that tragedy, to read the bureau's Annual Report of 1910 and 1911 is to marvel at the scope of its work, the extent of its investigations, and the breadth of its recommendations, all in record time. The section on runners is particularly revealing.

"Hardly have the men and women shouldered their bundles, gazing in bewilderment at the strange city, when from Battery Place and the surrounding streets there swoop down upon them, like a flock of hawks, runners, cabbies and confidence men," described one writer in 1916.

Running back and forth from docks to immigrant hotels to restaurants, runners "sold" the immigrants false hope in languages the immigrants spoke. The runners led the new arrivals to lodging houses, specific to their nationalities, for a fee; they took their luggage and only returned it—for a fee; they promised jobs—for a fee—but the jobs were rarely there; they sold five-cent rail tickets for fifty cents; they dressed immigrants like an American—for a fee—and they exchanged counterfeit dollars for the immigrants' real money. The bureau exposed the scams and recommended licensing runners, centralizing ticket sales at railroad terminals, other administrative changes, and emphasizing that the changes would only work with vigilant enforcement.

Not surprisingly, the bureau also focused on public work camps, inspecting 106 out of 167 statewide. They found American-born workers lived in "real" buildings complete with dining halls, but immigrant workers, each known only by a number, lived in jerry-built, rat-infested hovels without sanitation, sufficient heat, or edible food. The railroad camps were the worst, with filthy tin shacks built from materials found along the tracks.

The bureau discovered some 1,500 Greek teenagers living in 250 New York shoeshine parlors, working as indentured servants to pay back padrones, who claimed them as relatives to sneak them through Ellis Island. Flower peddlers were no better off.

Collecting facts and coupling them with advocacy, Kellor did not hold back in her analysis: greed, public apathy, and blatant discrimination caused the deplorable conditions, and she stated unequivocally that bad conditions bred bad behavior.

No form of exploitation "was more detrimental . . . than the colossal frauds now practiced on aliens in the sale of land," the bureau reported. Bogus real estate agents distributed pamphlets in the tenement neighborhoods of New York, celebrating idyllic towns with all the assets a new American might want: churches, stores, schools, and fertile land. They organized excursions to show "model" acreage to the travelers who, unknowingly, gave down payments on worthless deeds or lands. The victims could sue, but the fine was only $25—hardly worth the legal effort.

Other agents promoted contests, offering free land to anyone who successfully completed a simple puzzle and bought a similar piece of land next door, but the neighboring land was barren or nonexistent. Since the agent was not, technically, advertising fraudulent land, he evaded any laws.

"Once deceived, it is very hard to interest him [the immigrant] . . . and accounts, in some measure, for his investments [back] in his home country. There, at least, land sharks do not sell him ponds and sand pits and jungles for a home or a farm," wrote Kellor.

Many injustices occurred in other state agencies, and Kellor needed to exercise careful diplomacy, often calling for enhanced powers and resources for those agencies. When the bureau proposed increased fees or penalties on some powerful interests like employment agencies, private banks, steamship companies, and emigrant hotels, she faced their ire. But she persevered and, by 1912, the bureau's staff had doubled, and the multilingual staff tripled. Soon at least five other states moved to establish a similar bureau. And yet "the Lady," as she was now known, was discouraged.

NEEDED: A DOMESTIC IMMIGRATION POLICY

The Dillingham Commission, the federal commission that had, in part, inspired Governor Hughes's New York State Commission on Immigration, finally released its report in 1911. It made eight recommendations; seven focused on whom to keep out of America.

"To that small group of dreamers who had expected the promulgation of a domestic policy, who had waited for the constructive note, who had hoped that the Government might be urged to accept some responsibility which it now leaves to benevolence, the overwhelming negative position of the Commission is a disappointment," Kellor wrote in a widely circulated article. She reiterated that assimilation required employment opportunities, education, and protection from fraud and exploitation. Assimilation would never take hold if the government only focused on the immigrants and not on the prejudices and ignorance of native-born Americans.

THEODORE ROOSEVELT'S THIRD RUN AT THE PRESIDENCY

Kellor personified Progressivism: respect for facts, an interest in efficiency, and a deep belief in the common good. She also believed that the federal and state governments had to work together, and believed that Theodore Roosevelt's Progressive Party could do just that. In 1912, Kellor, at age 39, resigned from the bureau and, with Jane Addams, wrote the industrial and social platform including immigration for Roosevelt's third run for the presidency.

They waded deep into the roiling waters, calling for an "enlightened measure of social and industrial justice." The platform supported women's suffrage, union organizing, and the abolition of child labor. It supported minimum wages, the improvement of working conditions, and eight-hour workdays for women. And it denounced "the fatal policy of indifference and neglect which has left our enormous immigrant population to become the prey of chance and cupidity . . . We favor governmental action . . . to promote their assimilation, education, and advancement."

Roosevelt lost, but Kellor did not lose faith. She led the educational branch of the Progressive Party, asking Jane Addams, John Dewey, Gifford Pinchot, and other notables to direct separate research divisions to educate the public about a range of issues. She personally drove the work on immigration.

With a savvy understanding of communications, the education office distributed the results of its research through publications, slide shows, films, and speakers. It seeded state chapters to enact local legislation, but internal tensions with the political arm of the party grew; money was hard to come by, and keeping the grassroots engaged was difficult. In 1914, the service closed.

WAR TWISTED KELLOR'S AMERICANIZATION

In 1914, when war was declared in Europe, one third of all Americans were either foreign born or first generation, and most were touched, directly or indirectly, by the cataclysmic debacle engulfing the continent. Many young Germans in America wanted to return home to fight, and some mounted pro-German rallies. Others fiercely defended neutrality, even as pressure on America to fight the Germans increased. Anti-immigrant sentiment in America, already simmering, boiled over.

Frances Kellor, now founder and director of the nongovernmental Committee on Immigration in America, continued to argue that America would achieve national unity through education, assistance, and mutual respect.

"Americanization," wrote Kellor, "is a process, not of repression, but of protection and education of aliens and Americans—a process of free trade in a culture of reciprocity, mutuality and cooperation."

She knew she had to go big and public. The committee's most visible and metaphorical project, if not its most substantive, was the initiation of National Americanization Day on July 4, 1915. With the support of President Wilson and Theodore Roosevelt, she organized 107 cities to mount celebrations of citizenship.

The future Supreme Court Justice Louis Brandeis gave the keynote address in Boston, saying, ". . . we must not only give to the immigrant the best we have, but must preserve for America the good that is in the immigrant and develop in him the best of which he is capable . . ." In Pittsburgh, 10,000 immigrants listened to 1,000 children sing patriotic songs as the children formed a human American flag. In Indianapolis, recently naturalized citizens spoke in their native languages about the duties of citizenship. At a Ford assembly plant in Highland Park, Michigan, employees from multiple nations marched down a long runway into a mammoth pot that six teachers pretended to stir; from it emerged all the men wearing American clothes, waving American flags.

But by July 4, 1917, when America was in the war, even Theodore Roosevelt turned against reciprocal understanding, saying, "Unless the immigrant becomes an American and nothing else then he is out of place and the sooner he leaves the better."

Factories, public schools, settlement houses, and YMCAs offered English classes and civic lessons, but the line between assistance and coercion became thin. Henry Ford sent caseworkers to his immigrant employees' homes, checking their lifestyles and distributing incentive pay if the company approved of their lifestyles. When 900 Greek and Russian workers took the day off to celebrate Orthodox Christmas, Ford fired them, saying, "If these men are to make their home in America they should observe American holidays."

Native-born Americans asked difficult questions about split loyalties: Would non-citizens be dedicated to Americans and the Allies, or to the Germans? Who among them should be allowed to serve in the military? What if someone served who could not speak English? Would immigrants become spies?

Patriotic societies multiplied. A wealthy Chicago businessman established the American Protective League, officially endorsed by the US Department of Justice. It recruited thousands of volunteers in scores of cities to spy on potential traitors, judging loyalty through the superficial: attendance at rallies, singing the national anthem, taking anti-German oaths, buying liberty bonds. Other anti-German "patriots" burned German books and forced schools to stop teaching German. Some college professors were dismissed and employees fired for making what were construed as anti-American comments. One German-American on vacation in Florida was heard saying when it rained, "This damn country," and was arrested for treason.

Americanization took on a new and ugly meaning.

KELLOR'S NEXT AND FINAL CHAPTER

Postwar America was no better. Labor-management struggles escalated; the Red Scare, fueled by the Russian Revolution, blanketed many American institutions; and Congress passed numerous federal laws to exclude many immigrants, reduce their overall numbers, and ferret out would-be troublemakers.

Frances Kellor stayed active in several national immigration organizations, trying to coordinate educational activities with the federal government. She continued to write extensively, but she rejected the new interpretation of Americanization, believing that many efforts were "a noisy and futile hunt for spies . . . and many immigrants have come out of the war with a sense of resentment and, in some instances, bitterness." Kellor "left" immigration reform in 1921.

"A leadership not constantly in jeopardy loses its edge; and if not held on merit loses its power . . . It is possible we might have to wait

. . . for the full assimilation of the immigrant—for it may be that the full identity of interest consists less in sharing what money alone will buy, than in the mutual appreciation of the spiritual qualities of men."

Though Kellor left formal immigration reform, she did not "give up." In 1926, she was one of the founders of the American Arbitration Association. Litigation always ends with one loser and one winner on no common ground. Kellor and her colleagues sought an alternative. Two opposing parties—not unlike a new immigrant and a native-born American—could find common ground and mutual respect with the help of an intermediary. She stayed involved for thirty years.

Frances Kellor died in New York in January 1952 at age 78. She left no immediate survivors except for Mary Dreier. In one of the surprisingly few tributes to her, Sylvan Gotshal, a prominent lawyer and Jewish leader in New York, described her as "a combination of St. George and Joan. The dragons of doubt and the enemies of fear were laid low with a vision for the future no other eye beheld . . ."

AUGUST VOLLMER
The Insightful Creator of Modern Policing

November 4 in 1955 was a brisk but sunny morning in Berkeley, California—a good day to die. Gus Vollmer helped his housekeeper make his bed, sent her on an errand, called the police, went to his garden, and shot himself.

His many friends and admirers were distraught but not surprised. He was 79, a widower with no children of his own—only neighborhood kids who dropped by to solve their problems and eat his candy. He had lousy vision, Parkinson's disease, and debilitating arthritis, and he had just learned he had throat cancer. An active, endlessly engaged man, he would never be bedridden.

Tall and handsome, he was a friendly and decorous postal clerk when he was elected Berkeley Town Marshall in 1903, and later appointed police chief. He applied a scientific approach to the investigation of crimes and criminal behavior and the hiring and training of police officers. He introduced innovations that police departments nationwide adopted and still employ—from radio cars to crime labs. From that little town on the San Francisco Bay, Gus Vollmer became the father of modern American policing.

HIS EARLY YEARS

Born in New Orleans in 1876, he was the son of first-generation German immigrants. His father died when Gus was just a boy, and his mother raised him and his brothers alone. For two years, they lived back in Germany, their mother's native country, but then returned to Louisiana. Years later, FBI agents in California produced a classified list of suspected Nazi sympathizers that included Vollmer. The claims were roundly debunked.

When Gus was thirteen, the family moved to California, riding west with the widow of David Hennessey, the police chief of New Orleans who had been assassinated in the first "mob killing" in America. One of Vollmer's protégés wondered later if this encounter with the dead man's widow planted the seed of Vollmer's future interest.

In San Francisco, he worked in office jobs for six years before he and a friend began a coal and feed store in Berkeley. But when the Spanish-American War broke out, Vollmer left his business and joined the Marines, surviving 25 battles on a riverboat in the Philippines. Like Colonel Waring in New York, he returned home a war hero with deep admiration for the organization and meritocracy of the military. He also returned able to shoot a gun, a useful skill for a future policeman.

In 1905, the local civic leaders in Berkeley had grown tired of the gamblers, prostitutes, and opium addicts who crossed the bay from rowdy San Francisco. They approached August Vollmer and begged the postal clerk to run for town marshall. Reluctantly, he agreed, sure he would never win. He won with a three-to-one margin. He was 29 years old.

POLICING IN 19TH CENTURY AMERICA

Vollmer stepped into a national mess playing out at the local level. America, particularly its cities, was poorly equipped to handle the new challenges of urbanization, industrialization, and heterogeneity. City police departments were invariably weak, called by one observer "marvels of stupidity and corruption."

With departments often the handmaidens of the industrial class or the spokes of political machines, conflicts were rampant. In New York, the police department controlled the Board of Elections. In Philadelphia, the mayor appointed cops, and when the mayor lost an election, every police officer was fired. Denver had sixteen chiefs in twenty years, including an undertaker, a butcher, and a florist.

In spite of their political might, business elites grew increasingly concerned about social and economic disorder, and entire private security companies—Pinkerton, Wells Fargo Security, Rocky Mountain

Detective Association, and others—emerged. Granted police powers, they worked only for their customers—the railroads, banks, mines, cattle ranches, and mills. Everyone else depended on the local police.

Any man with brawn or a knack for politics could become a cop. Untrained and underpaid, a typical policeman was all too eager to take graft and wield his nightstick. The local cops were often hesitant to make arrests in their own neighborhood. With no cohesive philosophy or standard practice, and professionalism an unknown concept, chaos reigned.

THE BOY MARSHALL

In 1905, Vollmer began in a tiny office in the local firehouse with four deputies. Early on, taking a sledgehammer to the door of an opium den and destroying evidence, he lost the case. A quick study, he learned his first lesson: An arrest without verifiable proof is meaningless. The next time, he snuck into the opium den, waited until the action began, made arrests, and got his conviction.

Fame came quickly, although, perhaps, unwelcomed. Two notorious murderers who were wanted nationwide, Kid McMunn and Long Shot Harry Brush, slipped, unbeknownst to one another, into Berkeley to hide in the shadows of the small town. But Kidd McMunn was killed in a dramatic shootout, and Long Shot Harry Brush killed himself and his lover when Vollmer and his men surrounded his hideout. Overnight, Berkeley and its Boy Marshall became nationwide heroes.

Then in April 1906, an earthquake shook San Francisco and the resulting fires destroyed most of the city. Fifty thousand people escaped across the bay and Berkeley's population exploded from 20,000 to 45,000 in a matter of weeks. Fearful of increased crime, the city council allowed Vollmer to hire sixteen new deputies, and they maintained order. In 1909, when Berkeley adopted a new charter, allowing for the appointment of a chief of police to replace the election of a town marshall, Vollmer got the job. He stayed for 23 years and, from that perch, professionalized policing nationwide.

WISE MANAGEMENT AND CLEVER INNOVATION

Without a roadmap to show him the way, but with a reservoir of common sense, Vollmer first built a core of well-trained and honest cops. He used a new intelligence test to choose recruits, had a psychiatrist assess their emotional health, and began a mandatory 300-hour training program, the first in the nation.

He hired students from the University of California to work as part-time police officers. These "college cops" worked nights, patroling the neighborhoods, sneaking time to read their books under streetlamps; by the early 1920s, they made up one third of the department and won worldwide attention. Some stayed in law enforcement assuming senior jobs around the country—often hanging Vollmer's photograph in their offices—but even those who did not stay "set a tone and a new standard," explained one former college cop.

Vollmer challenged all the officers to think creatively. Take the case of the "unknown, naked, dead woman," wrote Vollmer. The chief turned to a medical doctor and a parasitologist who determined how and when she died, a psychiatrist who assessed what type of person might have murdered her, a chemist who evaluated her hydrated skin, an anthropologist who figured out her ethnicity, a shoemaker who determined that she was short and fat, and a dry goods salesman who figured out her height and weight. In addition, a mortician put eyes, ears, and hair on her corpse, and a photographer retouched her image. Knitting it altogether, Vollmer knew the victim was a crewmember of a Mexican train that had left Berkeley months earlier.

But effective policing also means smart patrols—not just sending any cop to any street. Like Colonel Waring, Vollmer assessed each residential and commercial area and calculated how much attention each area needed. He factored in time for investigations and arrests, and then assigned officers, based on their own interests and talents, to each area. Strategic deployment was born.

Non-ideological, Vollmer also grappled with crime prevention, debunking "well-intentioned but ill-informed" theories of crime reduction that denied the complexity of criminality. Ever the pragmatist, not a moralist, he did not believe increased penalties were morally wrong, just ineffective—and he opposed the death penalty throughout his career. He did not believe halting immigration, slowing down divorce, or building new playgrounds was wrong; he just found them naïve.

"All theories cannot be right and yet they may not be wholly wrong." But, he said, cops would prevent and solve crimes more effectively if they understood that criminals have different backgrounds, different preferences, and different styles. Without glorifying them, police officers needed to "cultivate the acquaintance of criminals." So every Friday, Vollmer brought pickpockets, gamblers, murderers, burglars, thieves, and safecrackers into headquarters to talk with the officers. His cops visited mental institutions; once, Vollmer, with sarcastic intention, had a phrenologist "assess" a bald detective by the bumps on his head. Vollmer interviewed criminals after their convictions and often stayed in touch with men who had served time. He considered *Criminals*, an analysis of the criminal mind, the best of his four books.

Vollmer's emphasis on recruitment and training culminated in the University of California at Berkeley's famous School of Criminology, the first of its kind in America, established in 1916.

AN EARLY ADOPTER OF TECHNOLOGY
AND SCIENCE IN POLICING

Some consider Vollmer's advances in personnel his most significant accomplishment. Indeed, by the mid-century, at least forty of his protégés were running police departments, teaching police administration, or working high up in federal law enforcement agencies. But his emphasis on applying science and new technology in police work was more dramatic and, to some, equally significant. The list of innovations defies imagination.

He was the first to put officers on bicycles, then on motorcycles, and then in automobiles. Although Vollmer never learned to drive, Berkeley became the first motorized police department in the nation. This was 1914, one year after Henry Ford began his assembly line. Later when someone suggested using radios, Vollmer responded, "If we could get radios into police cars it would be a monumental achievement." He did it and revolutionized policing yet again.

A voracious reader (a trait many of the leaders in this book share), Vollmer introduced the European system of crime detection to America. Using a standardized form, his officers described crimes in minute detail: Who was the victim—a rich older woman living in an elegant, three-story brick house or a corner grocery store in a rundown area; how did the criminal gain entry—through an open window, picking a lock, sweet talk; what did he steal—jewelry, money, bank notes; at what time did he commit the crime; what was he wearing? How did he arrive? Did he leave any trademarks behind, like cigar smoke or a polite note? The cops got to "know" a criminal by his MO, and luck gave way to analysis.

It all came together with a bomb scare.

Early one morning, a local man with gambling debts spotted a brown package in his garden. A long white string wound out from its side, burning slowly at the end. He cut the string, found sticks of dynamite, and called the police. The police spun the string in a centrifuge, analyzed the sediment at the bottom of each test tube, and determined the string came from a farm with Jersey cows, black and white rabbits, Rhode Island Red chickens, and sorrel horses. The farm was easy to find, and the farmer thought he knew who stole his dynamite. The police found the suspects, arrested them, and the first crime lab in the nation officially began.

Vollmer and John Larson, a college cop, discussed how changes in blood pressure might reveal a liar. Larson built an ungainly and heavy, six-foot-long contraption with wires, rubber tubing, a glass pump, and blackened paper strung between two spindles. He hooked Vollmer up to the machine and asked the chief some simple questions. Vollmer lied about his bedtime hour and his fondness for roast beef and the needle on the paper shot up. Dubbed the "lie detector" by reporters, the Berkeley Police Department used the polygraph regularly, solving burglaries, robberies, and a San Francisco kidnapping. Larsen married an innocent interviewee, and Vollmer eventually questioned the lie detector's reliability, if not the marriage.

VOLLMER'S NATIONAL INFLUENCE AND FINAL YEARS

One small department in one small city could not professionalize all police, but Vollmer understood the power of the press. He gave five local reporters permanent desks inside police headquarters with total access to all police files—no delays, no edits, no changes, no erasures. Their subsequent stories multiplied Berkeley's impact and heightened its reputation.

And times were tumultuous. All around the country, the burgeoning labor movement and the strong resistance against it incited violence; in a notorious incident in Boston, cops walked off the job, causing riots and bloodshed. Demands for police reform increased and Vollmer was called to advise cities from Dallas to Minneapolis.

In 1923, Vollmer took a formal leave of absence from Berkeley to run the huge Los Angeles Police Department. But its 1,600 cops tried to sabotage him, and Vollmer resigned in frustration with the continued graft and scant political support. He returned to Berkeley after just one year. Some thought it was a bitter defeat for him, but his reputation was strong. It was LA that looked bad. He remained in Berkeley.

In 1931, Vollmer wrote a scathing report on police departments for a federal report President Herbert Hoover ordered. Vollmer described incompetent and underpaid police officers with no training, discipline, or incentives to improve; he called for greater selectivity of police officers, improved benefits, and increased training and education of them; and he blasted the practice of rough third-degree interrogations. His national reputation was anchored.

The following year Vollmer retired from the Berkeley Police Department, but he did not slow down. He wrote extensively and taught at the University of Chicago and back at Berkeley, a high honor for someone who had only finished primary school.

Always organized and thoughtful, he planned his end just as he had lived. He willed his body to the Berkeley medical school and his house to his housekeeper; he destroyed all personal letters, lest anyone be hurt or insulted; and he indexed and donated all his papers to the University of California and the Berkeley Police Department. Then he killed himself. Today the highest point in the Berkeley Hills is aptly named Vollmer Peak.

LINDSEY, LATHROP, AND FLOWER
and the Twin Births of Juvenile Courts

Ben Lindsey was a tiny firebrand with a big heart. When he was 31 and a county judge, he found his path, and it led straight to kids. Lindsey listened as a railroad detective accused a boy of stealing coal. Hearing no rebuttal from the accused and with no available alternatives, Judge Lindsey sentenced the "trembling, wide-eyed boy whom I shall call Tony Costello" to the state reformatory.

"The air was rent with a scream that was to ring in my ears through all the years of my life," wrote Lindsey. "[T]he outcry of agony came from the toothless mouth of an old woman—the mother—arms waving in the air, shawl clutched to her breasts, face writhing terribly as she shrieked with anguish."

Stunned, Lindsey asked the district attorney if Lindsey could suspend the boy's sentence and assume responsibility for the boy himself.

"A stickler for the letter of the law, [he] had little sympathy with my ideas and he hesitated, but I did it anyway—as I have many times done since in the interests of justice," wrote Lindsey about an early sign of his anti-authoritarian proclivities. The DA said okay, and that night, the judge found the two-room shack in the poor Italian section of town where Tony and his parents lived. Years later he wrote:

"Sit down—if you can find a chair—and gasp in the foul air. Take a good look at that father over there, sick in bed from lead poisoning, a cast-off from the 12 hour-a-day smelters . . . See a whole family damned by poverty, going down in slow starvation . . . I talked with Tony and found him not a criminal, not a bad boy, but merely a boy . . . he had brought coal home from the railroad tracks to keep them warm. There was no glow within me as I left the home of Tony Costello. Instead, I carried with me something of the Costellos' view of my court and its absurd handling of their boy. I began to think over this business of punishing . . . and maiming young lives by trying to make the gristle of their unformed characters carry the weight of our iron laws and heavy penalties."

Within a few years of that encounter, Ben Lindsey was the most famous juvenile court judge in the country, rated in a national poll the eighth greatest living American, tied with Andrew Carnegie, the philanthropist, and Billy Sunday, the preacher. His dedication won him both fervent admiration and vicious enmity; the state of Colorado disbarred him in 1929.

BEN LINDSEY, THE BOY

Benjamin Barr Lindsey had a childhood of mixed blessings. Born in Jackson, Tennessee, on November 25, 1869, to a former captain in the Confederate Army and the well-to-do daughter of a plantation owner, he was one of four children. Loved by both his parents and maternal grandparents, Ben was, however, buffeted between them when his father, an intellectual dreamer, converted to Catholicism, much to the horror of his maternal grandparents. In 1879, his parents moved to Denver—perhaps to escape the family's disapproval. Ben was ten.

Denver was not like other American cities. A dry, treeless plain without a major river, it was settled when gold, then silver, was found in the three-mile-high, majestic Rocky Mountains that rose above it. "Mining the miners" was the fastest way to make money, and Denver's early roots were saloons, whorehouses, and gambling dens. Epitomizing the Wild West, Denver's first local law outlawed liquor sales on the streets, its first local tax was levied on saloons, and its first marshall earned fifty cents every time he arrested and jailed someone in his own hotel. But Denver soon had a core of wealthy and influential residents who championed the city with grand buildings, a well-respected newspaper, private clubs, and an aggressive Chamber of Commerce that promoted Denver as the Switzerland of America.

Young Ben did not spend his formative years in Denver, however. After one year in a public school, his father sent him to a boarding school attached to the University of Notre Dame in Indiana. Ben remembered the story of gentle St. Francis, the bigotry of some of the priests, and a persistent cloud of damnation that covered the school and its students. After two years, his father, having lost his good job in Denver, sent Ben and his brother back to Tennessee to live with their grandfather, who sent them to a Southern Baptist School. Ben adjusted.

In 1885, Ben returned to Denver and found his father sick and unemployed, and so, at sixteen, he went to work, never returning to school again. Two years later he found his father dead in their cellar, where he had slit his own throat with a razor.

Exhausted and anxious, Ben juggled menial jobs to help the family.

"Poverty was fraying us . . . it was warping us, breaking our health and ruining our dispositions."

And then, defeated by despair, young Ben, at age eighteen, placed the muzzle of a revolver against his forehead and pulled the trigger. His suicide attempt failed and many years later he wrote, "I went back to my life with something of a man's determination to crush the circumstances that had almost crushed me." Ben channeled his anger on behalf of other despondent and hopeless kids.

LINDSEY, THE LAWYER

Reenergized, Lindsey became a clerk in a law office and, thanks to the informal rules of the day, argued cases in court. At 24, he joined the Colorado bar and, with a partner, opened a small law practice.

Their first case was a malpractice suit. A young boy had broken his leg, but his doctor treated a bruised hip. Lindsey took the doctor to court, not once, but twice. Both times the trial ended in a hung jury. Determined to try the case a third time, Lindsey then had a visitor. Big Steve Stevenson, a political heavyweight with a waistline to prove it, urged Lindsey to settle the case out of court.

"We got eleven to one each time," Lindsey responded optimistically. "We'll win yet."

"You will, eh?" Stevenson laughed. "One man stood out against you each time, right?"

Lindsey agreed.

"Well, there always will be one. You ain't going to get a verdict in this case. You can't."

"Disinclined to drift into crookedness," Lindsey took—and lost—similar cases: a young man mutilated in a factory accident who received no compensation or the mother whose little boy was killed by a streetcar and was denied money because the boy's future financial worth was unknowable. Lindsey began to understand—the little guy was up against invisible powers that cared little for his troubles. At five foot five, weighing less than 100 pounds, Lindsey developed what he called "a burning passion . . . to fight for justice."

In 1890, a new compulsory school law gave Lindsey an opening. The law gave the state authority over all truants from six to seventeen years old, who were "unable to read and write . . . not engaged in some regular employment . . . a habitual truant . . . incorrigible, vicious . . . or who habitually wanders about the streets . . . shall be deemed a juvenile disorderly person . . ."

Lindsey convinced the district attorney to send all juvenile cases to his court, where, he said, he would help them become good citizens, not punish them for being bad. "Thus our juvenile court was begun informally, anonymously, so to speak, but effectively," Lindsey wrote, clearly driven by passion, not concept.

LATHROP AND FLOWER:
THE MOTHERS OF JUVENILE COURTS

Lindsey became the best-known juvenile court judge in America, but it was two women in Chicago, Julia Lathrop and Lucy Flower, who started the first such court.

Born in 1858 in Rockford, Illinois, Julia Lathrop attended Rockford Female Seminary for two years, where she met fellow student Jane Addams, the future Nobel Peace Prize winner. Lathrop transferred to Vassar College and, in 1880, having devised her own interdisciplinary course of study, she graduated. She was one of only 3 percent of college-educated women in America.

"A paragon of best behavior," as one historian described her, she returned home to work with her father, a prominent lawyer, but, in 1890, she picked up and moved to Chicago to live on the third floor of Jane Addams's Hull House.

The year before, Jane Addams and her friend and possible lover, Ellen Starr, had moved into a rundown mansion in an industrial part of Chicago where poor immigrants lived in crowded, unsanitary wooden houses. Inspired by her visit to the highly respected Toynbee Hall in London, Addams established Hull House, with a saloon on one side of it and an undertaker on the other. She did not start Hull House with any "preconceived social theories or economic views" about her endeavor other than building a "Cathedral of Humanity." She and Ellen Starr filled the house with furniture and art common in upper-middle-class homes, and then they invited their neighbors in for tea. Soon 25 or so educated women lived there, initiating programs and conducting groundbreaking empirical research.

"Hull House is rarely interpreted as a commune although it clearly was such an enterprise . . . As predominately unmarried professionals, they developed complex and intimate friendships, difficult to document because of their unrecorded daily interactions. These women wrote together, lived and ate together, taught together, exchanged books and ideas, vacationed together, became officers in each other's organizations, developed a pool of expertise on a wide range of topics and generated numerous changes in the social structure of government. There is no corollary among men," writes Mary Jo Deegan, a sociologist.

Julia Lathrop was one of its most distinguished residents. Empathetic and orderly, she had, as Jane Addams wrote, "a sense of moral obligation and unforced sympathy." Always prim in a dark blue suit, she was "a brunette but thought being blond would help her politically." With an intellectual rigor, Lathrop witnessed and documented the breadth of problems that defined the lives of poor people surrounding Hull House, particularly those related to child labor. In 1892, the governor appointed her to the Illinois Board of Charities, and from that platform, Lathrop inspected more than 100 orphanages, poor houses, mental hospitals, jails, and shelters in the state. "What must they have thought," wrote Jane Addams, "when . . . she tucked her skirts around her ankles and slid down a newfangled fire escape to see if it really worked."

Lathrop saw how police, courts, and jails often mistreated children, treating them like adults. Government, she thought, should act like a wise parent, not a punishing disciplinarian. Lathrop turned to the Chicago Woman's Club to find allies.

In the 19th century, upper-middle-class women, mostly wives of prosperous men, began to venture outside the comfortable confines of their homes. At home, they were placed on pedestals of respectability, responsible for the efficient management of the household and the morality of the children. Domesticity was an emblem of success, and women earned respectability and stature as protectors of their families and moral guardians of society.

Stepping out of those traditional roles into the civic sphere required breadth and curiosity, and women's clubs were often the vehicle. Reflecting the times, the clubs were often exclusionary with Protestants, Catholics, Jews, and African American women starting their own. They offered intellectual stimulation, social interaction, and charitable activities among their members. The Chicago Woman's Club was one of the most active.

Begun in 1876 for "mutual sympathy and counsel, and united in efforts toward the higher civilization of humanity," its original 21 members met in each other's homes, but it soon grew—with a clubhouse and club colors—providing lectures to its members on topics such as "The Influence of the Home upon Our National Character" and "How to Raise Boys." By 1898, its 700 members engaged less in literary and social pursuits, and more in "practical helpfulness." Given their traditional roles, it was natural for these privileged women to focus on health, education, and child welfare. Lucy Flower was one of the club's most influential members.

Born in 1837 in Boston, Lucy Flower taught in public and private schools in Madison, Wisconsin, before moving to Chicago with her husband, a prosperous lawyer. With three children at home—and servants to help—Flower joined the Chicago Woman's Club, serving as its president at one point. She established the city's first training school for nurses, a vocational school for dependent boys, and, as a member of the Board of Education, spearheaded the opening of kindergartens in public schools. She was even elected, as the first woman, to serve as a trustee of the University of Illinois—this without ever going to college and many years before women had the vote. And she was a donor to Hull House. Lucy Flower was a force.

KIDS IN TROUBLE AND THE CHICAGO JUVENILE COURT

Most children in cities were poor because most adults in cities were poor. Idle, the children often wandered, sometimes in neighborhood gangs, looking for food to eat, trinkets to sell, or coal to burn. Railroad tracks, boxcars, and garbage dumps were full of temptations. "The streets were not paved with gold, but junk," writes historian David Nasaw.

Police often picked children up for theft, arson, mischief, loitering, bad language, and vagrancy. In Chicago at the end of the 19th century, if a cop picked up a kid he took him (or her) to one of eleven different police courts. No court records existed and no coordination occurred among them. The judge knew nothing about any child he saw. Without legal representation or money for fines, and sometimes with negligent parents, many poor kids ended up in orphanages, almshouses, or industrial schools. If laws, however minor, were broken, judges sent delinquents to reformatories or "minor-jails for mini-adults," as one historian characterized them. Some young people ended up in dismal adult jails, not knowing how long they might be there. And the numbers were large. In 1898, Chicago arrested more than 15,000 people between 10 and 20 years old and 500 under the age of 10!

But the view of childhood was evolving. "Child-savers" saw children as developmentally different from adults, not responsible for their own transgressions, and needing protection and guidance. Often these reformers blamed the parents, sometimes society, and they pursued different avenues to save children from abject poverty, harmful neglect, and criminality.

The Chicago Juvenile Court was reflective of one such search for decency. Based on their shared view that children were different, Lathrop and Flower framed a social and financial argument for a juvenile court. They drafted the legislation, but, as women, they were barred from testifying at the state legislature, so they built support for it among men who could. They raised the money for it. They were successful.

The court opened in July 1899. Although the law did not differentiate dependents from delinquents, it defined court procedures for all juveniles, making the process more informal, less frightening; it centralized and maintained records so the judge would know if and why a young person had been to court before; and it separated young people from adults in institutions and barred children from adult jails altogether. For the first time, probation officers, not institutions, worked with juveniles. First and foremost, it was rehabilitative, not punitive.

The Chicago Juvenile Court also changed attitudes. Richard Tuthill, its first judge, urged police officers to "confer with parents, priests or pastors, using every effort to set the child right without resorting to an arrest, save as a final reserve." Now when a police officer brought a young person to court, a volunteer from the Chicago Woman's Club sitting next to the judge would tell the judge about each child, his home situation, and the charge against him. The judge could send the child home with a voluntary probation officer if deemed appropriate. (Eventually, the city paid for the probation officers and increased their numbers.)

In the first four months of the court's operation, 581 kids came to the court: 200 went to various institutions, but 381 were placed on probation. Within 10 years, 22 other states established juvenile courts. Julia Lathrop and Lucy Flower began the first one, but the speedy adoption of their innovation rests primarily with Judge Ben Lindsey, the "tiny giant."

LINDSEY, THE KIDS' JUDGE

If Lathrop and Flower started a juvenile court based on a philosophical perspective, Lindsey was all intuition. Perhaps it was his small stature, his childhood, or his big heart, but Lindsey had an uncanny ability to relate to kids. "Putting a little love in the law," he shortened the wooden legs of his bench so defendants could see him, and he ditched his black robe so as not to scare them. His approach was simple: If you are honest with me, I will be fair to you. Being fair meant respecting their world, and in their world kids did not snitch on one another. Lindsey expected honesty from them, but never asked them to rat on their friends.

He recruited truancy officers and volunteers to provide guidance to the kids, but, unlike Flower and Lathrop, who saw raising children as primarily a woman's job, Lindsey believed that fathers had a significant role to play, too. That might well have been a natural result of the traumatic loss of his own father.

In 1906, Judge Lindsey sentenced, on average, 186 boys and 6 girls to probation each month. Every Friday, he met with the girls, along with a clerk, and every Saturday morning, he met with all the boys in his care.

Kids report to the Judge Lindsey every Saturday morning.

"The boys assemble early, two or three hundred of them, of all ages and all sorts . . . small kids and big fellers . . . well dressed and ragged . . . thieves who have stolen bicycles and thieves who have swiped papers . . . toughs who have sassed a cop or stoned a conductor, and boys who have talked bad language to girls . . . It isn't generally known, and the Judge rarely tells, what a boy has done; the deed doesn't matter, you know only the boy, and all boys look pretty much alike to the Judge," wrote Lincoln Steffens for *McClure's Magazine* in 1906.

"'Skinny, you've been doing fine lately; you had a crackerjack report last time. I just want to see if you've kept it up. Bet you have. Let's see,' and the Judge opens his teacher's report. 'That's great. Shake, Skinny! You are all right, you are.' Skinny shines."

And so, it would go all morning long.

"I don't see how he does it," said a local man. "The little rats fairly swarm up here."

"Love, kindness, gentleness and patience mixed . . . with firmness will do more for a boy than all the cursing, abuse, nagging . . . at home, or the swearing, threatening, cuffing and sweating of the police station or workhouse," Lindsey wrote. In the first two years of the juvenile court, more than 200 kids voluntarily came to court, seeking help.

"You're a mighty little boy," Lindsey observed to one. "How did you find your way down here?"

"Well, most every kid I see'd knew the way," the boy answered.

Lindsey shunned state institutions as often as he could, but even when he resorted to using them, he did it his way. Police in Denver collected a fee for each conviction and another fee when they successfully delivered someone to an institution. To maximize their "profits," they sometimes kept people in jail until they had a group, collecting for each with just one trip.

That petty graft infuriated Lindsey, so he decided to send the boys on their own. He would give the boy his court papers and money for the train and send him on his way, with no police escort. That way, the young person suffered no shame, the judge benefited from their trust, and the police officer did not pocket unnecessary fees.

When the notorious troublemaker the Dare Devil Kid escaped from a local jail, the police caught him and dragged him in front of Lindsey, who sentenced him to a state institution. Then Lindsey told the Dare Devil Kid to get there on his own. Horrified, the policeman said the judge was wrongheaded.

"But why will I fail?" Lindsey asked.

"That kid has been in jail thirteen times," the policeman responded.

"Well, captain, did it ever occur to you that the jail has failed thirteen times?"

Within two years, Judge Lindsey sent 42 boys to the state's industrial school and each one showed up on his own; by the time Lindsey left Denver in 1927, only five boys had disappeared on their way upriver.

TAKING THE FIGHT OUTSIDE THE COURT

Lindsey often entered the ring with adults. His earliest bout came with the notorious, illegal "wine rooms" found in the back of many Denver saloons. Gamblers and whores plied their trades in these rooms, luring boys into games and girls into sex. Lindsey pleaded with the district attorney, the police chief, and the police commissioners to shut them down, but too many politically connected people enjoyed the not-so-hidden wine rooms and Lindsey was told again and again to ignore the problem. The police chief thought Lindsey "had gone nutty." Even his friends advised him to back off: "Don't get so excited . . . people will think you're not sane," Lindsey wrote of what he was told.

Frustrated, Lindsey invited the commissioners of the police board to his court one Saturday morning where the boys on proba-tion and reporters awaited them. The commissioners sat in the jury box as the boys told vivid stories from the witness stand about what went on in the "wine rooms."

"You knowingly permit the [wine rooms] in violation of the law. Yet the child is punished and disgraced. You and the dive-keeper, the real culprits, you go scot-free," Lindsey lectured the commis-sioners—as if they had missed the point of the show. The newspa-pers trumpeted the session, the local clergy picked up on Lindsey's theme, and powerful men in Denver were humiliated—and furious. It was only the beginning.

"Sometimes it is necessary to grandstand with a megaphone," Lindsey said, as he continually pulled out his bullhorn. He contin-ued to raise the issues, the public's support, and the powerbrokers' ire.

Before Lindsey had totally alienated the politicians, the state legislature passed his Juvenile Delinquent Law. The law stated: "[A]s far as practicable, any delinquent child shall be treated, not as a criminal but as misdirected and misguided, and needing aid, encouragement, help and assistance."

Like Chicago's law, it required a reporting system, provided paid probation officers, prohibited anybody under fourteen from being sent to an adult jail, and required separate detention centers for fourteen- to sixteen-year-olds.

For the first time anywhere, the law held adults accountable for a kid gone bad—the court could fine a negligent adult $1,000 or send him to jail for a year. In 1906 alone, Judge Lindsey heard cases against 725 adults, charged with selling liquor to minors, turning a

blind eye to prostitution, and other contributing factors to delinquency. These legislative victories won him, and the court, national
and international attention.

He received hundreds of letters from troubled parents, worried
teachers, and anxious children from all around the nation. Some
sent money, some begged for advice, many wanted his help. He answered them all. Eleanor Cramer, a former defendant, wrote Judge
Lindsey from her desk where she kept a framed photograph of him:

"Once upon a time in the year 1912 a very little girl wrote a very
big man about the very wonderful thing that happened to her because the very big man had come within her sphere and impressed
her very much."

International dignitaries sent emissaries to Denver to see the
court. Lindsey lectured throughout the nation, telling stories that
rallied the public. Walter Lippman, the famous journalist, wrote,
"By touching something deeply instinctive in millions of people,
Judge Lindsey animated dull proposals with human interest." And
the nation's most influential muckrakers befriended him.

LINDSEY, THE MUCKRAKER

As the nation's population soared, transportation multiplied, literacy
increased, and consumerism exploded, newspapers and magazines
proliferated. Finding new subscribers to bring in new advertisers
was key to the financial health of the burgeoning publishing businesses. Competition was fierce. What better way to entice readers
than to publish exposés of graft, corruption, greed, and collusion?
Consequently, many editors and hungry publishers hired journal-
ists, novelists, and even one biographer, Ida Tarbell, to go out and
"rake the muck."

Louis Filler, an American historian, offered this composite of
the typical muckraker:

"He was born in the 1860s, anywhere in the West—the Midwest
perhaps—where the pioneer had driven stakes and set about building a city . . . the boy was of good native stock of intelligent and

hard-working parents . . . he was soundly educated and . . . cherished literary ambitions . . . but drifted inevitably into journalism . . . enjoying a first-hand view of contemporary America, he was deeply impressed by the great factories and ships and railroads, the incoming droves of immigrants, the big city's slums, strikes, and wealth and poverty elbow to elbow. These things were far from literature, but they were life and they were real . . . This new America needed description and explanations and maybe even reform; it was a bad, splendid America; a serious, farcical, gaudy, unsophisticated America, seething with new thoughts and new problems."

In turn, the wide distribution of magazines and newspapers dramatically increased the muckrakers' reach. "It now became possible for any literate citizen to know what barkeeps, district attorneys, ward heelers, prostitutes, police-court magistrates, reporters, and corporate lawyers had already come to know in . . . their business," Richard Hofstadter, the historian, writes.

The muckrakers gravitated toward Lindsey, who had many stories and few inhibitions. Jacob Riis, the Danish photographer of the slums of New York City, became a lifelong friend and introduced him to President Theodore Roosevelt, who publicly endorsed the judge's vision of juvenile justice in 1904. Lincoln Steffens, the endlessly curious son of a California banker and the author of the incendiary *The Shame of the Cities*, wrote glowingly about Lindsey in his book, *Upbuilders*: "His courtroom equals the State, Law, Justice, Home, School, Club, Society, Friendship, Success . . . it is the place where Failure goes for Help and Hope renewed . . . Lindsey didn't just establish another institution, but injected humanity into those institutions."

Upton Sinclair, author of the hard-hitting expose of the Chicago meatpacking industry, became a loyal fan, once even organizing newsboys nationwide to donate pennies to Lindsey when the judge faced a fine for refusing to testify against a boy caught up in legal wrangling. And it was Sinclair, the avowed socialist, who urged *Everybody's Magazine* in New York to publish Lindsey's personal story of Denver's corrupt judicial system.

Denver powerbrokers tried to stop the publication, delivering to the New York editor forty pages of papers describing Lindsey's "political trickery, treachery, judicial unfairness, favoritism, demagogy, and . . . lunacy, degeneracy and degrading immorality."

The editor sent a reporter to Denver to interview ministers, priests, rabbis, teachers, lawyers, parents, and newspaper publishers. *Everybody's Magazine* ran Lindsey's tales with a note from the editor, saying, "Judge Lindsey was as honest as he was brave; he would not lie about his worst enemy."

In the series, and later the book, *The Beast and the Jungle*, Lindsey blasted corrupt courts and political elections:

"Instead of being a contest of parties . . . [it is] a contest of corporations . . . The 'workers' in the ranks were working for nothing . . . the politicians were struggling for . . . the offices and the graft . . . the corporations were . . . using them to keep themselves above the law. And the people? In none of the private conversations do I remember hearing the people mentioned."

He named names, revealed financial kickbacks, outlined employment realities, and described knowing winks between the powerful and the police. "Beasts," he wrote, "hide in the tangled underbrush of government and corporations—and when they spring from the forest they are all powerful." Denver's corporate titans and political elites were furious.

LINDSEY'S THIRTY-YEAR WAR

Lindsey's fiercest defender was his wife, Henrietta Brevoort, a blonde, blue-eyed socialite from Detroit. They met in 1913 when they were both "patients" at the Battle Creek Sanitarium, an upscale health retreat. They married the same year, without her parents' knowledge, and soon adopted a little girl, whom they named Benetta. In 1915, Henrietta became Lindsey's assistant—nepotism that today would be frowned upon.

"Neither his friends nor his enemies suspected she had the spirit of Napoleon," wrote Helen Strauss in the *Missouri Monthly*. "It is doubtful if Lindsey knew either." But in her work, Henrietta encountered unwanted babies, abused wives, homeless people, and neglected children, and "traded comfort for reality." She always stood by Ben's side and the fights were fierce.

Lindsey got in the middle of the infamous Ludlow Massacre of 1914, one of the most violent uprisings in the history of America. Coalminers struck at the large mine, and the Colorado National Guard, at the behest of John D. Rockefeller, the owner of the mining company, shot cannons and Gatling guns into the miners' camp, slaughtering the men and their families, including eleven children.

Spurred on by Upton Sinclair, Lindsey led a delegation, including miners' widows and their children, to meet with President Woodrow Wilson in Washington, DC to protest the actions. Calling the massacre "a struggle between property rights and human rights," Lindsey kept hammering nails into his own professional coffin back in Colorado.

The Ku Klux Klan emerged as another formidable foe. In the Colorado elections of 1924, the Klan, targeting Jews and Catholics, ran candidates as Republicans, won every statewide office, and took control of one house in the state legislature. Lindsey, an outspoken critic of the Klan, squeaked to victory with an atypical tiny margin—137 votes—and his Klan opponent challenged the result in court.

Right in the middle of this legal battle, Lindsey published *The Companionate Marriage*. Focused, as always, on the best for children, and perhaps enjoying the limelight of controversy, Lindsey went on a national book tour. He argued that young married couples should use birth control—although contraception was illegal—and, if the couple proved incompatible, they should consider divorce before children were born and hurt by the disruption.

The national uproar came from every corner of society: Catholics, Protestants, middle-class and working-class people alike. Lindsey publicly called the pope absurd and police forcibly removed him from a large church in New York when he got into a screaming match with an Episcopalian bishop. With virtually no support among the justices on the Colorado Supreme Court, he lost the election challenge back in Denver. Judge Lindsey was ousted from his court. It was 1927 and he was 58.

"Self-righteous people are sadistic," wrote William M. Houghton in *Judge Magazine* about Lindsey. "Hounded out of office and denounced from the pulpits of the nation, it doesn't do to disappoint the Christians."

Exacerbating the situation, Lindsey, his wife, and two staff members, followed by reporters, piled into their cars, drove to a Denver dump, and burned all the juvenile court records in a gasoline-fueled bonfire. Outraged by his smugness, the establishment was not through with Lindsey yet.

In 1929, Lindsey received cash from a friend whom he had advised—not represented—in her New York divorce case. Citing laws against judges accepting gifts, the Colorado Supreme Court disbarred him. Judge Ben Lindsey, the dedicated, albeit undiplomatic, juvenile court judge, could no longer practice law in the state of Colorado.

"Suppose that instead of being disbarred, you had been elected a Supreme Court justice. I would have had to suspect you had gone crooked or that all you ever said was bunk. As it is, you are disbarred and all is well; all is as you said it was; and as I said it was. The Beast has got you," Lincoln Steffens wrote.

Lindsey and Henrietta left Denver and moved to Los Angeles.

THE FINAL CHAPTERS OF LATHROP, FLOWER, AND LINDSEY

Lucy Flower stayed vigilant and helpful with the juvenile court, but it was her last crusade in Illinois. In poor health, she and her husband moved to California in 1902; she died there of a stroke in 1921 at age 84.

Julia Lathrop's career, however, soared. President Theodore Roosevelt had tried and failed numerous times to get Congress to establish a federal Children's Bureau to research, coordinate, and lead on issues related to children. In 1912, after Roosevelt was

JULIA C. LATHROP

gone, Congress approved the establishment of the Children's Bureau, and President William Howard Taft appointed Lathrop its director—the first woman ever to lead a federal bureau.

She arrived in Washington, DC knowing that the federal departments of education and public health believed that they were the ones to protect America's children, not the nationally known social worker from Chicago. Lest she make unnecessary enemies in bureaucratic turf battles, Lathrop proceeded quickly but carefully, focusing initially on "Why Babies Die?" The bureau educated the public about maternal and infant nutrition—a neutral but winning strategy. Later she focused on more difficult and contentious issues, such as child labor, but not before she won the support of congressional leaders for the Children's Bureau in general.

Lathrop often worked collaboratively with others, but, interestingly, she never invited Lindsey to participate in any of the work of the Children's Bureau. He had once, in his rash and undiplomatic way, called social workers "scientific robots, jabbering always of records, statistics and standards." Furthermore, Lathrop believed Lindsey was a press hound—not something she practiced or admired.

Lathrop stayed for nine years and then returned to Rockford, Illinois, her hometown. From there she traveled to Europe on several occasions, representing America as a global ambassador for child welfare and social justice. She died in Rockville in 1937, just shy of 74 years old. She never married.

Ben Lindsey served as a superior court judge in Southern California, wrote, lectured, and saw a few minor bills passed, but his fellow California judges, perhaps resentful of his boasting or maybe horrified by his open discussions of birth control, never made him judge of the juvenile court. But infatuated with Hollywood glamor, the Lindseys socialized with the famous, dined with film stars, and stayed close to Aimee Semple McPherson, the famous radio preacher. In 1935, when the Colorado Supreme Court reinstated Lindsey into the Colorado bar, the couple decided to stay in Los Angeles. The judge died there of a heart attack in March 1943. He was 74.

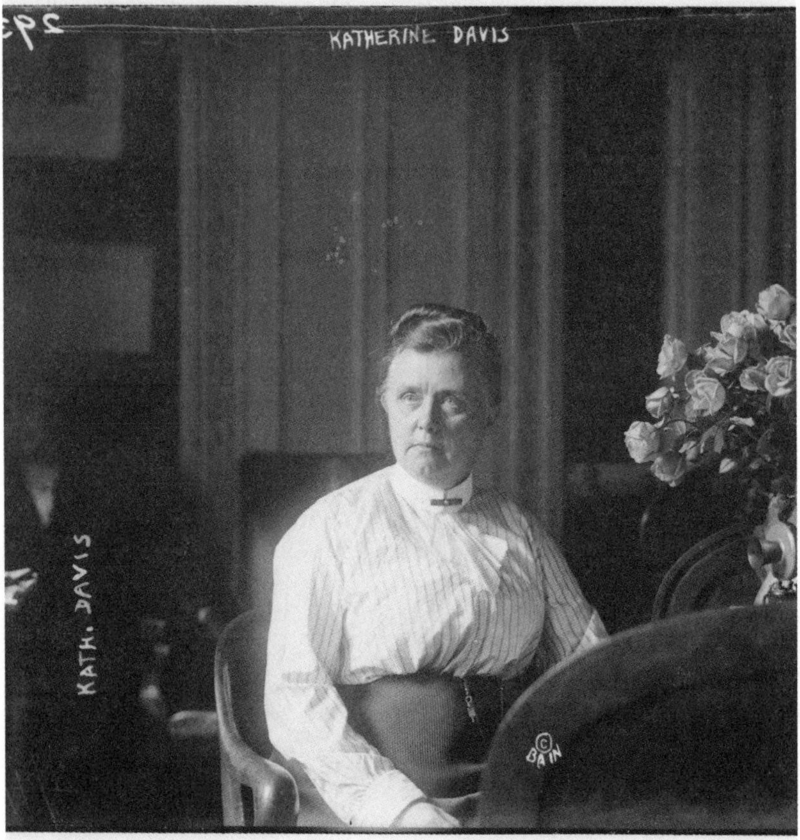

KATHERINE DAVIS
KATH. DAVIS
© BAIN

KATHERINE BEMENT DAVIS:
The Protective Scholar of "Wayward" Women

B elle Moore, a 25-year-old, rail-thin, biracial woman, nick-named the Mulatto Madame, was a real pro. In 1910, when she was arrested in New York for selling two young women to a brothel in Seattle, she had been running whorehouses for more than nine years. In the much-ballyhooed case (the first for procurement), Belle testified that the young women had consented and were over seventeen, although their teddy bear and doll belied that last claim. Belle, who had received $120 for the transaction, got two to five years in prison.

There was nothing new about prostitution in New York—or anywhere for that matter. What was new was its proliferation as young single women poured into cities. Its visibility grew and the graft between police and operators exacerbated it. Prostitution be-came big business and a national obsession.

Everyone had an opinion: George Kibbe Turner, walking the sex beat for the hugely popular *McClure's Magazine*, maintained that prostitution was the byproduct of too many saloons that needed side businesses to survive. Emma Goldman, the socialist activist, argued that underpaid and mistreated female factory workers were forced into prostitution by unjust economic conditions. Others blamed political machines with corrupt police departments in their cogs, while preachers bemoaned the changing morality of society—the looseness of young, primarily immigrant girls at dance halls. Others impugned Russian Jews and Southern black men for run-ning the "white slave trade." The hysteria was deafening.

In response, John D. Rockefeller Jr., the philanthropic son of the founder of Standard Oil, was asked to chair a grand jury to investigate whether a white slave trade existed in New York. After months of work, the group of 23 white men, assisted by investigators, declared that no organized sex ring existed, but that prostitution was rampant and the prevention of it was a pressing problem.

Rockefeller and Katherine Bement Davis, the warden of Bedford Hills Reformatory for Women, teamed then up.

LIFE BEFORE PRISON

Katherine Bement Davis, the oldest of five children, was born on January 15, 1860, in Buffalo, New York, to an accountant and a suffragette, herself a daughter of one of the original feminists at Seneca Falls in 1848. (Katherine Bement Davis always used her entire name in recognition of her grandmother, Rhoda Bement.)

The family moved to Rochester, where Katherine finished high school and then, having inherited her father's talent for numbers and analysis, taught chemistry and math for ten years before enrolling at age thirty as a special student at Vassar College in Poughkeepsie, New York, in 1890. Davis did not participate in extracurricular activities there, but when she graduated in 1892 Phi Beta Kappa, she spoke at the commencement and served as "Class Grandmother" at the celebratory dinner.

She moved to Brooklyn to teach chemistry at a girl's high school and further study nutritional chemistry, but a Vassar professor, remembering Davis's organizational skills, recommended her for management of the construction and operations of New York State's exhibit at the Chicago World Exposition during the summer of 1893.

The exhibit, designed to demonstrate how "domestic economy" could stretch limited working-class budgets, was a little two-story shingled house with green shutters and planted window boxes. Davis managed its construction, detailing everything from the costs of all construction materials, furniture, and clothes to the sample daily menus, complete with their nutritional benefits. "The little

Model of New York Working-man's House, 1893

house at the big fair" drew thousands of visitors, and Davis welcomed them all.

With a manager's touch, a scientist's precision, and a humanist's concerns, her professional trajectory began to turn. She moved to Philadelphia to administer the city's new College Settlement House, modeled after Hull House in Chicago. Young college graduates, mostly women, paid to live in poor neighborhoods, in this case an African American area, to learn firsthand the realities of poverty and the skills of a social worker—this before any school of social work existed.

Paid $800 a year (the equivalent of about $22,000 in 2018), Davis managed the programs, which were as broad as the area's needs. She built new houses and protested the physical conditions of local tenements. She organized black mechanics, excluded from trade unions, and she hosted W. E. B. Du Bois and his wife, who lived at the settlement house, as they conducted scores of interviews for Du Bois's first book, *The Philadelphia Negro: A Social Study.*

But Davis knew what she did not know (a trait she shared with other municipal innovators) and, in 1897, she returned to graduate school. The University of Chicago, founded only five years before by John D. Rockefeller, was already in the vanguard of progressive thinking. With the advent of so many scientific and industrial advances, people—particularly reformers—venerated facts. Before, presumption was reality: The unemployed person was a vagrant, the ill person was ignorant, the prostitute immoral. But data strengthened policy arguments, justified programs, and enabled evaluation. Respect for the collection and analysis of data became a hallmark of Chicago's approach to study, and Davis, with her scientific and mathematics background, was a strong and experienced proponent of this approach.

At the University of Chicago, she took a range of courses; studied with Thorstein Veblen, the eccentric economist and harsh critic of American society; and explored German agricultural economics while living with a family and perfecting her German.[1] She received her PhD, cum laude, in political economics.

THE START OF PRISON LIFE

The new Bedford Hills Reformatory for Women on farmland forty miles north of New York City sought "a woman of constructive imagination, capable of understanding her material, and creating something to meet its needs . . ." wrote Ida Tarbell, the crusading journalist. A professor at the University of Chicago recommended Katherine Bement Davis, "an exhaustless source of cheerful energy," and, in 1900, Davis arrived as its first head, intent on giving female offenders a second chance.

After overseeing the construction of six new buildings, in May 1901, Davis welcomed the first inmates. They arrived—sixteen to thirty years old—"battered and worn," uneducated, poor, often covered in lice, sometimes mentally unstable, and stayed for up to three years. Workhouses and reformatories for women (with female staff) existed, but few, if any, were well managed, and Davis, a scholar with strong managerial instincts and a thirst for understanding, became one of the nation's foremost leaders in prison reform.

Few women committed serious crimes in those days; a few notorious murderers, like Lizzie Borden, belie the reality. Most incarcerated women had not hurt people; they had offended society, committing crimes of moral turpitude. They were prostitutes,

---

[1] Known for his love of women but his hatred of students, Veblen advertised his office hours at the university as Mondays, 10–10:05 a.m.

vagrants, drunks, or petty thieves. The proverbial fallen woman, who toppled from the pillar of the ideal, was considered a blight on society. Considered threats to the social order, even the root cause of male criminality, women criminals were thought to be irredeemable, and they were rarely a focus of 19th century prison reform. Consequently, they were mistreated.

Sometimes jailed with male inmates, they were raped by guards or other inmates and sometimes impregnated. Invariably crowded into small and unventilated spaces, they suffered beatings and the horror of leg irons. In one notorious case, a woman was set afire in her cell. Wayward women were considered fair game, playthings of sadistic guards in an unsupervised system.

But as more and more women—primarily educated, upper-middle-class, white women—exercised their talents outside the home in the abolition, suffrage, and temperance movements, some focused on prison reform and the rehabilitation of women inmates. Davis was one of those. She began at Bedford Hills with the strong belief that respect breeds good behavior.

"Each girl will . . . understand [that] her standing will depend, not on her past record, but wholly on her conduct while here." She greeted each new inmate with tea and chocolates and a new gingham dress and white apron. "Why she even let us use her best silver spoon," said one inmate.

The women lived in cottages with progressively more independence and responsibility, depending on their records. They farmed the land, cooked the meals, and cleaned the buildings, often with Davis at their sides. Few had any education, and Bedford Hills offered schooling. No fences or walls surrounded Bedford Hills, and in ten years, only four girls escaped.

But Davis was not a pushover. Neither "the sentimentalist who wants to idealize the criminal . . . [or one] who regards the criminal as a beast with no possibilities in him," wrote one newspaper article. She sometimes used handcuffs and sent unruly or violent inmates to the disciplinary house.

Ever the analyst, Davis, the warden, approached Rockefeller, the moneyed moralist, to seek support for a unique research center at

Bedford Hills to study the inmates and their motivations. With his financial support, her staff interviewed, assessed, and then tracked 1,000 of Bedford Hills' former inmates—something never done before. Three quarters were released within two years—one year earlier than expected—which told Davis that Bedford Hills was doing something right. Of those, 52 disappeared and 154 broke their parole, but 393 did well, marrying or holding down legitimate jobs. From this research, Davis grew to understand that some, primarily the mentally ill and developmentally disabled, should not have been in prison in the first place. She would fight for and eventually win funds to build a separate facility for such women.

ROYAL AND PAPAL TRIBUTES

Davis had been at Bedford Hills for eight years when she took a much-needed vacation by herself to the ruin-rich island of Sicily. Eager to see the limestone caverns in the seaside town of Siracuse where, 3,000 years before, Athenian soldiers were jailed, she was there on December 28, 1908, when a massive earthquake struck north of her.

Coupled with a towering tsunami, the disaster instantly killed some 100–200,000 people in Sicily and Italy and flattened, washed away, or burned more than 90 percent of Messina. International ships, alerted by telegraph, rushed to Messina to ferry traumatized survivors to safety—including 4,000 half-naked and wounded people, who staggered off ships into Siracuse, a town 100 miles to the south that had one small hospital and no trained nurse.

Davis immediately extended her stay and, with permission from the local mayor, began organizing relief operations. Using funds from the American Red Cross and the same competence and sensitivity she demonstrated at Bedford Hills, she hired local women to sew underwear and clothes, paying thirty cents a day plus lunch; she hired men to cobble shoes, sizing them according to when the wounded individuals were due to be released from the hospital. She opened an orphanage for children who had lost both parents and another for "half-orphans." And she started a convalescent home as others built permanent housing for the refugees. When she left three weeks later, saying she felt as if she were "leaving a large and helpless family," both the king of Italy and the Pope in Rome thanked her personally. She returned to America a national hero.

NYC DEPARTMENT OF CORRECTIONS

On January 1, 1914, the young, newly elected reform mayor of New York, John Mitchel, appointed Katherine Bement Davis, age 54, commissioner of corrections—the first woman ever to manage a city agency. A Presbyterian-turned-Congregationalist who never married, Davis moved from Bedford Hills to Jackson Heights, Queens, and lived with her two unmarried sisters in a cooperative apartment there.

Her appointment caused quite a stir. Some anti-suffragists said it proved women did not need the vote to gain power. The mayor replied that her appointment had nothing to do with politics and everything to do with Bedford Hills and Sicily. And Carrie Chapman Catt, the famous suffragist, led a parade of decorated cars down Fifth Avenue to deliver flowers to their honored colleague on her first day on the job.

In typical language of the day, the *New York Times* wrote, "She is plump and has an attractive, but not at all what would be called a pretty face; it is rather colorless . . . with light hair which is of no particular color, brushed tightly back . . . Davis is trimly dressed, thinking more of utility than how things look . . . there is nothing masculine about her . . . she is a woman with an air of comfortable womanliness."

Davis inherited a system in disarray—"the worst," she said. Young, first-time offenders were in cells with seasoned criminals; scant medical care was offered in severely overcrowded institutions. The department with 650 employees and 5,500 inmates in nine facilities was seriously underfunded, with just $2 million annually. Referring to Colonel Waring's tenure sixteen years before, Commissioner Davis said Corrections deserved more money than snow removal.

Prescient, Davis feared riots at Blackwell's Island, the largest prison in the system with "vile conditions, unfit for a pig." In July,

Commissioner Kate Davis on Blackwell Island

she was proven correct. A few prisoners smuggled cocaine into the prison, aided by guards, and when the warden discovered it, he punished all the inmates, who subsequently "ran wild." They cut power lines and set fires, protesting the warden and his unfair discipline. The prison went into lockdown, with inmates relegated to their cells with only bread and water and the ringleaders sent to solitary confinement. Upon hearing about the trouble, Davis went directly from a formal dinner to Blackwell's Island.

". . . I am a woman . . . [but] I am not soft and don't propose to be soft. I'll have order over here if I have to call out the militia, and not one of you will get a personal hearing until the whole lot of you make up your minds to be orderly," she declared as she marched through the cell blocks, dressed in her finery.

She met inmate representatives at a makeshift office, spent the night on the island, and the next day preached at three different religious services, accepting the repentance of some, but steadfastly refusing to excuse their earlier infractions. She summoned a judge to hear the case against the troublemakers; she filed formal charges against the doctor who had smuggled in drugs; and later she fired abusive guards.

"You have dismissed a fellow Progressive," one colleague said.

"I don't know if he was a Progressive, but I do know he was a drunk," Davis snapped. "I don't think a man's politics are any of my business."

Throughout her tenure, she often appeared unannounced at facilities to gauge their conditions, including a well-publicized late-night visit onto Hart's Island looking for knives and other contraband. She subsequently prohibited visitors from bringing anything into the prisons. She eliminated prison stripes and stopped tours, believing both degraded inmates, and she ended the corrupt practice of allowing inmates to "buy" better cells from correctional officers. She instituted a classification system so that murderers no longer shared cells with petty thieves, and she sent juveniles to a farm outside the city.

Continuously attacked by Tammany Hall critics, the press, and some judges who considered her reforms "fads," she did not shy away from explosive issues, including her steadfast refusal to separate black from white inmates, the common practice in US prisons. "An institution should be conducted on the character, conduct and needs of the inmates, not their color, race or religion," Davis said. And, as always, she insisted on accurate and coherent recordkeeping. One newspaper commented simply, "If this is feminism let's have more of it."

PAROLE BOARD

Along with the shift away from corporal punishment to constructive rehabilitation, indeterminate sentences became a key prison reform too. An inmate was more likely to change behavior if he could earn early release for good conduct, but it was politically and administratively difficult for one judge alone to determine an inmate's readiness for early release, so parole boards began at the state level. Davis was an enthusiastic proponent.

"The average offender hates the indeterminate sentence. He would much rather know in advance just what time he is in for, and then sit down and chalk off the days, instead of exerting himself to win free time by industry and good behavior," she said.

In December 1915, New York City established the first municipal parole board in the nation, and Davis resigned as commissioner of corrections to become its chair. She no longer ran prisons, managed hundreds of employees, or controlled a big budget. Taking a job that others considered "beneath" her to advance principles she embraced is another characteristic she shares with some municipal pioneers (Waring's street cleaning, Vollmer's college cops).

For two more years, she and two other members heard hundreds of cases, assessed their prison reports, interviewed inmates, evaluated their records, and granted parole to many. She resigned in 1917 when Mayor Mitchel, the reformer, was defeated in his second run for mayor.

BACK TO THE BEGINNING

"A woman of rare mental endowment, combined with a large heart, deep sympathy and an unusual amount of common sense," John D. Rockefeller Jr. wrote of Davis. Without his father's instincts for business or the jugular, but with an abiding interest in research and philanthropy, Rockefeller aggressively advanced many of the social reforms of the early 20th century with his father's money. After Davis left city service, he hired her to lead his new Bureau of Social Hygiene. With a staff of social science researchers, she focused on many aspects of vice from delinquency to dance halls.

But the project that consumed much of Davis's time was on female sexuality itself. She had seen too many young women in prison who did not understand the implications of seduction nor understand their own desires. Davis favored sex education but knew that society could never develop sensible principles for sex education or understand and prevent "deviant" sexuality if it did not understand "normal" sexuality. She recommended such a study.

The Board of the Bureau resisted such a radical idea: It's not within the Bureau's mission; animal biology is more important; the social sciences are not really science; it will embarrass us. They had many reasons to object, but Rockefeller did not stop her and Davis embarked on a seven-year project.

With advice from a prestigious committee, Davis and her colleagues structured two different surveys, but reaching a large sample was challenging. They used the only lists they could find, alumnae associations and women's clubs—undeniably a middle-class sample. They sent the two surveys to 20,000 married and unmarried women around the country—this before computers, Excel sheets, postage and copy machines, or SurveyMonkey.

The surveys asked about personal happiness, sex, contraceptives, masturbation, and homosexuality. Rockefeller's lawyer, Paul Warberg, wrote that "the questionnaire is an amazing piece of work . . . its frankness takes my breath away," adding that he would like to run up and look at the responses!

But in 1927, before the report was completed, Raymond Fosdick, one of Rockefeller's trusted associates and future head of the Rockefeller Foundation, convinced Rockefeller to fire Davis lest the bureau be irreparably harmed by her study. Rockefeller agreed, allowing Davis to finish the research but forcing her to resign and giving her one year's severance pay of $3,500. (Many years later, Fosdick wrote a biography of Rockefeller and did not mention Katherine Bement Davis.)

"I shall submit with, I hope, good grace to your decision and will not need to be carried off the stage kicking and screaming," Davis wrote to Rockefeller. And she did stay on the high road, even through her retirement dinner for 300 people at the Waldorf Astoria, where glowing toasts, including Rockefeller's, flowed with the champagne.

Two years later, Harper published *Factors in the Sex Life of Twenty-two Hundred Women* by Katherine Bement Davis. With the same detached tone and exactitude of all her academic and administrative work, Davis, some twenty years before Masters and Johnson's work on sexuality, reproduced detailed charts with facts felling old shibboleths: women enjoyed sex, almost half had "spooned" before marriage, frequent intercourse did not lead to infertility, and more lesbians came from coeducational colleges than all-women colleges. The book, without any promotion, became a bestseller.

By the time of its release, Davis and her sisters had moved to California, where Davis died of heart failure at 75 in 1935, five years after the Bureau of Social Hygiene closed its doors. Today some criminologists and feminist historians know about Davis, but a woman—declared in 1922 one of the 23 most influential women in America—who changed expectations for women in prison, helped bury Victorian myths, proved female competence, and accepted personal thanks from a king and a pope, has been lost to history. Katherine Bement Davis, with her ever-inquisitive mind, would undoubtedly ask why.

ELLA FLAGG YOUNG:

First in Her Chicago Class

The glorious Auditorium Theater of Chicago, with arches of gold leaf and walls of intricate mosaics, hosted symphony orchestras, opera companies, and even presidents, but no event matched the night of June 3, 1910. That night, every public school teacher and principal in Chicago, all 6,000 of them, arrived in streetcars, horse-drawn carriages, and on the El to honor Ella Flagg Young, superintendent of the public schools. The first woman in the nation to lead a major school system, in just one year she had brought peace to a troubled system. She always said respect for capable teachers was the key to children's success, and they loved her for it.

At 8:30 p.m., with some people in plush boxes, others in chairs on a platform built over the theater's floor, and hundreds more standing in the lobby and galleries, the orchestra played the majestic overture to Richard Wagner's *Tannhäuser*. Then 250 teachers—two from every school, elected by their peers—marched in pairs down the center aisle to stand in a semicircle at the foot of a raised platform in front. Ella Young, dressed in white satin, entered to thunderous applause and walked alone under a canopy of long-stemmed red roses that 200 school children—girls on one side, boys on the other—held aloft. Smiling, with a hint of tears in her eyes, she reached the dais, climbed the stairs, and stood listening to a song, sung to the Illinois state anthem, written in her honor:

Who's our type of woman noble?
Mrs. Young, Mrs. Young!

Friend in sunshine and in trouble,
Mrs. Young, Mrs. Young!
Standing firm to guide and sway,
Never once to halt and stay,
Progress, mounting day by day,
Mrs. Young, Mrs. Young!
Progress, mounting day by day,
Mrs. Young, Mrs. Young!

Afterward, Ella Flagg Young, refusing a seat, stood and shook the hand of every person in the theater before the dancing began. The tribute was "an expression of a better era . . . but beyond that it was a personal tribute to Mrs. Young, the woman, Mrs. Young, the educator, and to Mrs. Young, the delightfully human personality," wrote one observer.

Three years later, the Board of Education fired her. The reaction was immediate and ferocious and, under extreme pressure, the board reinstated her, only to resist her every move until she resigned for good two years later.

But Young's prestige locally and nationally did not come from her martyrdom. It came from her relentless devotion to the idea that all children, no matter their background, should discover their own talents and shape their own ideas with the help of well-trained teachers, and from her capacity for translating that commitment into action.

HER EARLY YEARS

Ella Flagg was the youngest of three children. Born in Buffalo, New York, in 1845, she was the daughter of Scottish Presbyterians. Her father, Theodore, was a meticulous sheet-metal worker who had little education but endless intellectual curiosity. An avid reader of history, current affairs, and science, he imbued Ella with a lifelong eagerness to learn. Indeed, throughout her long career, she reserved three nights a week for her own study, often inviting teachers to her home to join "the Ella Young Club."

Theodore often read books that contradicted the dogma of his church, and Ella remembered the lively but civil debates between her father and others about existential matters. Open and frank with Ella, he encouraged curiosity and inquiry—a practice that Ella drew on consistently as an educator. If "blood will tell," Ella's intellect came directly from her father.

Her mother, Jane Reed, was equally open to new ideas. Although religious, she allowed dancing, card playing, and theatergoing, contrary to Presbyterian orthodoxy. "She believed that religion should not be so strict as to drive young or old from the home to find amusement," Ella said when she later defended art in schools, mocked by many as an unnecessary "fad."

Ella was a sickly child, and her parents kept her from school lest she further harm her health; there she learned the useful skills of tending a garden and running a household. "My mother's mind was practical and forceful in business details, and from her I learned to face situations squarely," she said.

Ella also spent hours watching her father at the forge, questioning his processes and learning math. "I had manual training before such things were thought of, especially for girls," she said. Later Ella, as superintendent, believed that combining vocational skills with academic pursuits was healthy for all children, no matter where their futures might lead.

When Ella was about nine, she taught herself to read. It started with a newspaper article. A tragic schoolhouse fire both horrified and entranced her, and she insisted on hearing the article several times. She then took the newspaper and, from it, figured out the letters, the words, and the sounds, and taught herself to read. Soon she memorized much of the New Testament, could recite all the psalms, and surprised her mother by quoting extensively from a Calvinist preacher whose book she found in her father's library. The next day her mother took her to the library in town and borrowed *Tales of Mother Goose* to replace the other tome.

To practice her reading, she struck a deal with her older brother, Charles. Every day when he returned from school, they went to her garden together. He weeded and she read aloud, pausing for his questions or her own contemplation. From these afternoons, she said, she learned to be clear and concise, never pretending to know something she did not understand.

At eleven, she began school and soon became the monitor with a desk next to the teacher. Her father, sensing a hint of "priggishness," asked the teacher to put Ella's desk back down among the students. Years later, some people found Young severe and inflexible, but nothing in the records suggests a continued "priggishness."

When Ella was thirteen, the family left declining Buffalo for booming Chicago. The city with 100,000 people was defined by lumber and grain, and soon railroads and meat processing too. Ella began her final year of grammar school, but, bored, she dropped out; her parents did not object.

In 1860, she passed the teacher certification examination, but, at fifteen, she was too young to teach in a public school, so she enrolled in the Normal School, a new two-year teacher-training course for elementary school teachers. With little status, even lower pay, and often little support from parents, teachers were often a sorry lot—inept or desperate. In one Chicago two-room school, the director received $50 a month for supervising his daughter, who taught without a certificate, and his son, who served as janitor. In another, the director was illiterate; and in yet another, the teacher spent his days in the tavern.

States established Normal Schools to address the shortage of teachers, but that was not the same as advancing good teaching. Although Ella studied—philosophy, chemistry, astronomy, English, and pedagogy—she was never expected to probe the reasons for things, question orthodoxy, or think.

"She had a fairly good mind to start with, but if she continues under such teaching she won't have any mind after a while," her father said. Ella herself later wondered why she was such a willing student of such mindless teaching.

Ella's mother worried that Ella, hard on herself, might be too hard on her future students, and wondered if Ella should reconsider becoming a teacher—although in 1860, few, if any jobs, were open to women. Rather than take offense, Ella tested her interest and visited schools—not something expected as part of her training.

Most schools, public or private, were one-room affairs in houses, barns, railroad depots, or, if lucky, a stand-alone wooden structure. Not yet compulsory—that would not begin in Illinois until 1883—classes ranged anywhere from five to 120 students of different ages, usually with just one teacher. Sometimes two big students sat with three little ones in double seats; sometimes students came in shifts. Daily attendance varied dramatically, with children staying home to help their parents or unable to walk miles through the bitter cold or deep snow of Illinois winters. All schooling ended at eighth grade.

None of Ella's classmates at the Normal School were interested in visiting schools, so Ella went on her own, walking miles to different schools. Her first few visits were discouraging, but then she found a gifted teacher and returned repeatedly, observing her classes and watching how the relationship between the teacher and the students mattered enormously—a realization that shaped Ella's approach to education for the rest of her life.

In 1862, Ella Flagg began teaching for $250 per year ($6,000 in 2018 dollars) at one of the few large schools in Chicago. She was 17 years old and one of 17 teachers for 1,300 students. She volunteered to teach a class of rambunctious boys who herded cattle most days and caused trouble in school on other days.

"We took to each other," Ella said simply.

In 1865, a new superintendent hired Ella Flagg to establish the first two "practice" rooms at the Normal School; second-year teachers-in-training observed strong third- and fourth-grade teachers and then practiced what they witnessed. In two years, 176 students graduated from what was then considered the best Normal School in the nation.

Her work was not without challenges. Members of the Board of Education—political appointees, rarely educators—often expected her to enroll a friend or a relative. She resisted, refusing to lower her standards and believing that talent can be developed, but not given. Sometimes she even expelled people, no matter their connections. In 1871, the Board of Education took that responsibility away from her, and she resigned.

CHICAGO GROWS

When Ella Flagg Young began to teach, 110,000 people lived in Chicago; when she became superintendent in 1909, Chicago had more than two million residents. Cities were seductive. In the early days of industrialization, for every person who left the city for a farm, twenty people left farms for cities. Cities enticed farmers off the land for jobs, money, and fun. And the jobs they found had never existed before—factories, shipyards, railroads, slaughterhouses, and stockyards. They worked in conditions foreign to them and lived with people alien to them. The filthy streets, the crowded tenements, and constant disease were the price of hope.

Single women, widows, divorcees, women of color, and immigrants found jobs in the city, too. They worked primarily as domestics or in factories or, sometimes, on the streets. They worked long hours for little pay, no benefits, and, if hurt, no compensation. The plight of these poor women—and the plight of their children— became the focus of middle-class women, who entered the social realm to pursue civic and charitable work or, in some cases, teaching.

They entered a cultural maelstrom. In 1910, three quarters of all Chicago residents were immigrants and their children. Poor, they lived in densely packed enclaves, bringing with them their own traditions and experiences. Many were illiterate and unskilled, dark-skinned, and not Protestant. "Original" Americans feared they'd be outnumbered. Anti-Catholicism was rampant. Chinese immigrants were blamed for opium dens, and Germans and Irish for alcoholism. Eugenics, the theory that genetics determine behavior, was a commonly held belief, even among Progressives. One of its many proponents, E. A. Ross, a well-known sociologist, described immigrants as "armies of barbarians." *Wop, kike, dago,* and *guinea* entered the vernacular, and ugly, blatant nativism was common and accepted.

As the population grew and mechanization changed the nature of work, people began to value education more and to change their understanding of childhood. Children were no longer seen just as little adults needed to work the land. Calls for public education grew louder, and in 1883, the state of Illinois passed a law mandating that all eight- to fourteen-year-olds attend school for at least three months of the year. This put logistical and pedagogical pressure on the educational system.

Six years later, Chicago annexed several towns, adding 35,000 more students, 785 teachers, and 100 separate buildings to an already large system. Most of these urban schools were as poor as their rural counterparts, cramped with no light, no plumbing, poor ventilation, and untrained teachers, and rote learning and birch rods were standard. No coherent theory of education existed, and entirely too much political influence did.

"Schools can no longer be the silent halls of dark and mysterious book lore for the few . . . but are to become living, striving social groups where the young learn the parts they are best fitted to play," Ella Flagg Young wrote.

PRINCIPAL AND ADMINISTRATOR

She was offered a principal's position without taking the exam required of male principals. She said thanks, but no thanks, I'll take the exam. She aced it. The superintendent pronounced her principal "by right and not by courtesy," and the Chicago Board of Education changed the rule for good.

". . . a little bit of a woman, all vim, push and go-ahead . . . My, how she could make those boys fly. She with her jet-black hair parted in the middle, combed back smooth, and her clean olive skin and even white teeth. She always dressed in black, very plain. And her eyes, such eyes that looked you through and through," remembered one former pupil.

Respected as a strong manager, Young collaborated with the teachers and, as her father had done with her, encouraged them to develop their own approaches.

"No one can work in another's harness," she repeated.

Always interested in the latest theories about pedagogy, she was equally interested in the teachers' views, never imposing her beliefs on them. She expected results, but not conformity. "What new ideas have you today?" she regularly asked teachers.

John McManis, an early historian of the Chicago public schools, wrote that, "although her expression was somewhat severe when in repose, when . . . she became interested in the explanation of a lesson, her face lighted up . . . and became . . . almost beautiful."

Maybe severe, but opposed to corporeal punishment, she was strict with disruptive students. She had a knack for differentiating between rowdy noise and creative commotion, appreciating and encouraging the latter.

"Her power to know what was going on within the school was uncanny," said one teacher.

Sadly, these were personally difficult times for Young. Her mother and her brother, Charlie, had both died. She married an old family friend, William Young, but he died of respiratory failure in 1873, the same year both her father and sister died of pneumonia. At 28, Ella Young was alone. Ironically, she had trouble expressing her own emotions, but her empathy for others was never questioned, and teachers and administrators were rock solid loyal to her.

Within three years, she was principal of a much larger school. She went with a clear set of principles: Avoid regimentation among teachers and students, encourage spontaneous exploration and discourage passive learning, expect depth and breadth of thinking, and instill democratic principles of equality in the schools themselves.

To entice students to come to school, Young taught herself the mechanics of steam heat to ensure warmth in the frigid Chicago winters; she moved furniture to maximize light in the classrooms and insisted on opening the windows to ventilate the classrooms. She established one of the first school libraries, a debate society, and a mini Congress, and added gym, singing, and art for everyone. The mayor said she built the most effective social agency in the city, and in 1887, she was tapped to be the assistant superintendent of the entire system, responsible for improving teacher quality. Ella Flagg Young was 42 years old.

TEACHER QUALITY DURING TUMULTUOUS TIMES

She rode streetcars and the El all over the city, visiting schools, coaching the eager, and improving the weak. "The careless, slipshod shirker found little satisfaction in [her] visits," wrote one observer. Weak teachers called her "cold, hard, severe" and, in a popular insult of the day, "even mannish." But many others were inspired, sitting on stoops eagerly waiting to sign up for her teacher training classes.

"She stimulated us . . . to a greater intellectual curiosity and a new sense of the significance of intellectual life . . . she managed to give the doubter courage," wrote one member.

But these were tumultuous times. The nascent women-led teachers' union was gaining ground, questioning the salaries and working conditions of teachers. Fierce debates ensued about the role of schools. Should they prepare the future working class in just technical skills? Were their budgets justified? Why weren't the "three R's" sufficient? After all, they worked in the past and they were easier and cheaper to teach than these newfangled "fads" like music, art, and gym.

Her boss, the superintendent, had limited power politically and, inadequate resources administratively. Then Joseph Meyer Rice arrived on the national scene. Trained as a doctor, he became interested, initially through physical education, in the entire question of school performance. Over several years (1890–1893) he visited 1,200 schools in 36 cities. He noted the appearance and tone of the classrooms, the interactions among students and teachers, the nature of the schoolwork, and the usefulness of meetings. He then published a series on the sorry state of America's schools.

"It is incomprehensible that so many loving mothers are willing without hesitation to resign the fate of their little ones to the tender mercies of ward politicians, place them in rooms unfit to breathe with teachers who treat them with a degree of severity that borders on barbarism," he wrote.

His report on Chicago was devastating. A few excellent schools existed, but the overall system was disgraceful. He cited the low standards for teachers, many not even high school graduates. He described classrooms where children read one book over and over. He heard group recitations of inaccurate facts and suffered through constant rote memorization. He heard one teacher scream, "Don't stop to think. Tell me what you know!" He described another who taught "expressive reading" by having all students tilt their heads in nine set ways to express nine separate emotions:

Heads down! "Oh, all my money is gone."

Heads to the right shoulder! "You can't fool me."

Chicago schools, Rice wrote, were "mechanical, antiquated and absurd." The Board of Education vehemently disagreed, insisting that only 20 out of 3,500 teachers were inadequate, but Ella Flagg Young, the assistant superintendent, agreed.

"I cannot deny the testimony of my own eyes and ears," she said.

In June 1899, a new superintendent arrived, centralizing what little authority the position had and cutting the teachers out of school management. Young told a reporter she disapproved of his actions and then, embarrassed by her own indiscretion, she resigned.

The chairman of the Board of Education, faced with the fury of the Chicago teachers, tried to convince Young to stay, writing, "she is a woman of rare talent, untiring energy, large acquirements and ripe educational experience . . . I deeply regret her withdrawal." But Young declined to return. Hers was not an angry act, but an honest one—she understood the prerogatives of authority.

OFF TO THE UNIVERSITY OF CHICAGO
AND THERE, JOHN DEWEY

Professor John Dewey arrived at the University of Chicago in 1894 to direct the philosophy and pedagogy department and cement his reputation as one of the foremost philosophers of his time. Assistant superintendent Young began taking his weekly seminar and over the next four years studied logic, ethics, metaphysics, and Hegel with him. Their classroom rapport was enviable.

"There was no indication of . . . the sort of egotism that bores one to death. It was rather, if anything, a case of her and Dewey discussing Hegel to the neglect of the rest of us," wrote one classmate.

When she resigned from the Board of Education, the president of the University of Chicago invited her to teach at the university, saying he would waive the requirement for a college degree. Young—totally in character—objected, saying she could not ask teachers to pursue higher education if she did not have a degree of her own. Harper gave her time to study while she taught at the university. Graduating magna cum laude, she then completed a doctorate at age 55, arguing in her dissertation that children do best with hands-on learning in democratically administered schools.

Dewey opened a laboratory school on campus to test, evaluate, and then spread new ways to teach elementary school. It started small, but grew quickly. Dewey appointed his wife, Alice, as principal—a move that fueled already bad feelings about him not so much for the nepotism, writes educational historian Michael Knoll, but for her weak managerial skills and chaotic approach to education.

Dewey then asked Ella Flagg Young to come aboard. After all, she had done in schools what he was advocating. She brought coherence to the chaos, and for the next five years, she and Dewey tested and shaped what became known as Progressive Education.

Not easily defined, progressive classrooms—invariably more informal and individualistic than traditional classrooms—shaped curriculum around each student's physical, psychological, and intellectual capacities and interests. Arguing that a less authoritarian classroom would enhance democratic participation, Dewey and Young believed that school is life, not preparation for life. Dewey, who had scant experience with classroom teaching, wrote later of Young, "I would come to her with these abstract ideas of mine and she would tell me what they meant."

While always respectful, if somewhat exploitative, of Ella's ability to shape practice around principle, Dewey made numerous enemies on campus, particularly with other professors and the head of the other experimental high school on campus. When John and Alice Dewey left Chicago for Columbia University, Young wrote President Harper, saying about the mess, "Never in my life have I been in an entanglement like this." President Harper thanked his counterpart in New York for taking Dewey off his hands.

Young then took a year off and traveled in Europe, returning to Chicago to become head of the latest incarnation of the Normal School. She stayed five years and prepared more teachers than the system could handle.

THE POLITICS OF BEING SUPERINTENDENT

In 1909, all hell broke loose in Chicago public schools. A new superintendent and the Board of Education grappled with conflicting funding priorities, textbook selection, and difficult real estate decisions. The superintendent gave merit increases to teachers, based on evaluations the teachers never saw, and then he lied about the numbers. The union went nuts. He resigned in a storm of controversy, accepting a lucrative job with a textbook company.

Over five months, the board considered 27 candidates—all men except Ella Young. Several board members refused to support a woman—any woman. The lone female on the board pushed the issue and insisted that they interview the top five candidates including Ella Young. The candidate with real rapport with the teachers, extensive experience, formidable intelligence, and tireless commitment, Ella Flagg Young became superintendent, the first woman ever to manage a major school system.

"I only wish Ella Young was a man," said one board member. To cover themselves, the board authorized a position for a deputy superintendent and appointed a man to fill the slot.

Congratulations poured in about Young's appointment, however. "I regard Mrs. Young as one of the ablest educators in the United States . . . every element in the public schools of Chicago—particularly the men—should rally in her support," wrote the superintendent of the New York schools—the only system larger than Chicago.

Now responsible for 290,000 students, 6,300 teachers, 267 buildings, and a $12 million operating budget, Young moved quickly. Within the first year, she won approval for a massive building program to ease the overcrowding. She eliminated the secret marking system and increased teachers' salaries; she established teachers' councils to advise on books and curriculum, reducing possible graft; she pushed for turning the Normal School into a four-year college; she ordered the airing out of every school several times a day; and—it is said—she learned every teacher's name.

Her days were full of long-term policy decisions, conflicting priorities, and deeply divisive issues from the global to the granular. Opposed to vocational education, fearing it would typecast poor and immigrant children, she introduced manual arts into some schools, mixing the academic with the technical. Concerned about poor students, she mandated simple grey graduation costumes so that all could afford one, and began a school lunch program. She involved the schools in eradicating flies, a major public health challenge, and once even encouraged students to help the police find a missing girl.

She encouraged field trips, handicrafts, and dramatics. When a principal suspended 26 pupils for joining a fraternity (which were forbidden by the school board) to raise money for a senior prom, Young overruled the decision, saying, "After all they are only kids and they are fighting for what they think is right." No wonder they threw a big party for her.

Problems with the Chicago Board of Education simmered, however. The members fought calls from the union for pensions, which Young supported. They resisted her call for clear procedures for buying or renting land. Her opposition to separate vocational schools for those deemed unsuitable for academic study infuriated some, and others objected to her educational "fads."

She confronted religious bigotry. Many believed that Catholics put papal authority over loyalty to America and "accused" Young of being a Catholic. She went public to deny it:

"They say from one end of the country to another that I am a Catholic . . . I am a Presbyterian. . . . but for me to come out in the papers with this announcement would indicate there was something disgraceful about being a Catholic . . . yet it is said that I go to early mass . . . have an altar in my room and a son from a Catholic priest."

Most infuriating, the board second-guessed all her educational decisions and tried to wrestle control over content from her. The final straw came over textbook selections in reading and spelling. Some board members with obvious financial conflicts pushed certain textbooks, a major expense for the schools. Ella Young resigned. It was July 1915.

"Someone whose grammar isn't any good tried to tell Ella Flagg Young how to teach spelling," fumed one observer. The mayor intervened and Young agreed to return. At the next board meeting, however, a duplicitous board member nominated the deputy as superintendent and forced a vote on the board. With a 10-to-10 split, Young resigned, saying, "Any Superintendent, who needs more than one ballot to be elected, has not the support, and I therefore withdraw my name."

Her friend, Margaret Haley, the dynamic head of the Chicago Federation of Teachers, said, "Ella cried enough tears to wash away all the sins of the world."

The next day, the *Chicago Defender*, the major newspaper run by African Americans and a loyal supporter of her reforms, ran Ella's statement on its front page: "I could fight for a principle. I could fight for another person, but I will not make a selfish fight for my own position."

Reactions were swift and strong. Even the mayor—whom Young once suspended from school—publicly apologized for the male appointees on the board, saying that "the men that I appointed [should] resort to what I consider underhanded methods . . . to use the language of the streets, got my goat." The lieutenant governor suggested students strike; teachers announced they were joining the suffragettes so that they could vote in future elections; Margaret

Haley released the names of board members who had pressured Young to fire certain teachers; and people signed petitions to reinstate her. In a raucous and angry meeting, the Board of Education capitulated and voted unanimously to reinstate her. Young returned yet again for one year, a year full of continued misery.

Some board members boycotted meetings in silent protest. The Board of Education approved a massive deficit and accused Young of mismanagement, two board members were accused of graft, and members continued to fight Young on curricula policies. Young retired for good on January 1, 1916, at the age of 71.

"I violated one of my pet theories and I have always regretted it . . . I thought the members [of the board] meant what they said, but I was mistaken. If I had not gone back I should have escaped all the trouble."

Her farewell dinner was held in the same auditorium as the first tribute.

"The vast hall was jammed, not with people to see a show, but with solid citizens bent on showing their confidence in the City's foremost educator and on righting the wrongs done by politics," wrote John McManis.

Then, without fanfare, Ella Flagg Young moved to Los Angeles. She wrote about education, visited schools, and stayed involved with the National Education Association. In July 1918 at the NEA's annual convention in Pittsburgh, hundreds of delegates gave her, once their president, a standing ovation. Two months later, Ella Flagg Young died during the Spanish flu epidemic. She was 73 years old.

McManis wrote that if Ella Flagg Young had been a man, she could have "managed a corporation, run a railroad, commanded an army, governed a state." Undoubtedly true, and certainly meant as a compliment, but what Ella Flagg Young wanted to do mattered as much: give children a chance to discover their own talents and their own interests in an open and welcoming school. She succeeded on her own terms.

MELVIL DEWEY.

DEWEY, CARNEGIE, AND BLUE:

The Rise of Public Libraries— White and Black

Obsessed with efficiency and time, Melville Louis Kossuth Dewey hated his name; it was too long and too complicated. Mel Dui was much better. But the local bank refused to recognize his preferred but not formal name, so he settled on Melvil Dewey, with just one "L" in his first name.

Even as a little boy, he fixated on order: He alphabetized his mother's spices, reorganized her pantry, and rearranged his father's shoe shop. He learned shorthand to speed things up and so hated unnecessary letters in English words that he became a leader in the simplified spelling movement.

"The English languaj is . . . illojical, unsyentific, unskolarly . . . it addles peopl's brainz," he wrote.

Most significantly, however, Melvil Dewey became the nation's leading proponent of public libraries—well organized, well stocked, and open to all.

Before then, with few exceptions, libraries were small and exclusive; books were expensive to publish and education was a privilege. Ben Franklin opened a subscription library in Philadelphia in 1732, buying 46 books in England with funds collected from a handful of subscribers. Occasionally, an enterprising person bought books and lent them out for a fee; these circulating libraries popped up in newspaper offices, hat shops, even saloons. Colleges had libraries, but usually just with reference books, and some churches maintained small religious collections.

Social libraries, open only to select members, became the most ubiquitous new model; by 1875, there were an estimated 2,200 of them. These libraries, usually dominated by educated white men, encouraged intellectual and social discussions, and reflected—and insisted—on the values, interests, and behavior of their elite members. Their librarians, if they had any, were invariably members of the same privileged class, often scholars there merely to preserve and protect the valuable books.

Women were excluded from most of these social libraries, but as they became more educated, they sometimes established their own social libraries—often equally exclusive. By 1860, when the literacy rate among black people was a tragic 5 percent, free African-Americans had opened 50 social libraries throughout the northeast.

Some cities, like bustling St. Louis, had some of each: subscription, circulating, and social libraries. But in the mid-1800s, things began to change. As new printing techniques made publishing faster and far less expensive, the number of books and periodicals exploded. Typewriters and electric lights made reading easier, and railroads made distribution far simpler and cheaper. Compulsory education increased literacy, and a middle class with more leisure time emerged. Many began to see libraries as an essential supplement to formal education and a possible stabilizing influence on the emerging and rambunctious working class. A few even saw maintaining libraries as a logical role for government.

In October 1876, when 103 librarians met in Philadelphia to establish the American Library Association, there were only 188 free public libraries in America, and 127 were in Massachusetts alone. Melvil Dewey, age 26, went to that meeting with his newly conceived Dewey Decimal System in hand and the future motto for libraries in his head: "The Best Reading for the Greatest Number at the Lowest Cost." The modern public library system began.

DEWEY'S BEGINNING

One of five children, he was born on December 10, 1851, in a tiny town in north central New York State. His parents tightly embraced hard work, social responsibility, and moral certitude in an area permeated by social and religious reformers—evangelicals, Utopians, Seventh Day Adventists, Jehovah's Witnesses, abolitionists, temperance workers, women's rights advocates, and, in Dewey's hometown, argumentative Baptists.

Never particularly religious himself—he had little patience for endless debates about Scripture—he once joined a Congregational Church in Boston, primarily to meet young women. But these tempestuous times had an impact on Dewey the reformer. He developed what one biographer calls "aggressive self-righteousness." Once Dewey identified his "world's work," his devotion blinded him like the revivalists in upstate New York.

Coupled with his obsessive tendencies, everything for Dewey was about enhancing order. His messianic compulsions often offended people. Brash, he ignored other people—even those who agreed with his mission—and he always knew best. He manipulated situations and, worst of all, he sometimes acted as if rules or propriety did not apply to him. Regularly harassing women, he was eventually drummed out of the American Library Association. Dewey was a complicated, unlikeable genius.

He attended school in his town of Adam's Center and later in Oneida and graduated from Amherst College in Massachusetts along with 65 other poor but talented boys. One summer, he distributed Baptist pamphlets to rural families and saw the woeful lack of books. Consequently, as a college student, he worked in the library and, after graduation, stayed on as the assistant librarian for two more years. Never having been a strong student, what captivated him about libraries were their administrative and technical challenges rather than the content of their books.

DEWEY'S DECIMAL SYSTEM AND OTHER OBSESSIONS

Librarians, protective of their precious books, shelved them—away from readers—by title, sometimes by subject, sometimes by author, sometimes numerically. No standard method of organizing collections existed until Dewey had an epiphany. Number 10, his favorite number, was the solution.

With help from Amherst professors, he divided all general knowledge into ten 100-point buckets by subject: philosophy, theology, natural sciences, and so forth. He further divided each bucket by 10 into subcategories: History, for instance, became 900, European history became 940, English history, a subset of European history, became 942, Norfolk English history 942.6 and so on. Dewey published a technical guide to the system; once applied, librarians organized books sensibly in a coordinated way and readers could find books on open shelves.

He moved to Boston, where he juggled several of his obsessions and inventions; he began the American Metric Bureau, pursued simplified spelling reform, edited the new *Library Journal*, and managed the membership dues of the ALA. He rolled all these efforts into one account, not for his own gain (he rarely took much salary), but because they strengthened one another. Money from one paid the debts of the other. Ads, for instance, for metric materials in the *Library Journal* reached potential adopters, but the Metric Bureau did not pay for the space, so the *Library Journal* lost revenues. Dewey kept his investors and colleagues unaware of his convoluted business practices, but these accounting irregularities, and lack of transparency, eventually hurt his reputation, as would his interactions with women.

TRAINING AS A NECESSITY

Established in the mid-1700s, Columbia College (now University), venerable and proud, had seen its library fall behind other comparable institutions, so the board invited Dewey to build it up.

Offered a handsome $3,500 annual salary (about $85,000 today) and assurances that he could start a school of library science, Dewey, now 32, jumped at the chance and moved to New York with his wife, Annie.

They had met at that first ALA meeting in Philadelphia. She was the librarian at Wellesley College. They had much in common—her family was religious, and he had grown up in the New York Bible belt; his father made boots, her mother made shoes. And they both craved order. Each month they set personal goals for themselves. Dewey vowed to ride horses three times a week, dress better, eat slower, breathe more deeply, sing more often, and handle his money better. At the end of the month, they graded each other on their success. Loving his intensity—and probably his good looks—Annie always defended him, even when he inappropriately hugged and kissed women at an ALA meeting.

At Columbia, Dewey did what the college wanted. He enlarged its collection, consolidated separate collections, and reclassified all the books. He modernized the library in little ways, too, from adding brass stepladders on the open stacks to offering ice water for the patrons.

But he also alienated his colleagues. Pugnacious and often insulting, he did whatever he wanted to do, no matter whose toes he crushed. When a mathematics professor questioned Dewey's purchasing decisions, Dewey snapped that if the professor expected equity, he should go find the money himself to buy books.

He set out to change librarians too. In his inimitable way, Dewey described "old" librarians as "keepers of books, preserving them from loss . . . and worms." As promised by the college, Dewey started a school of library science—the first one ever. "Librarians must care for books, organize books, choose books, suggest books and encourage reading . . . The passive has become active," he wrote. He developed a curriculum, identified lecturers, and recruited students.

"The natural qualities most important in library work are accuracy, order (or what we call the housekeeping instinct), executive ability, and above all earnestness and enthusiasm," he said. Library work, he added, was less strenuous than teaching and "more effective" than the ministry. Dewey believed that women made ideal librarians, but Columbia did not enroll women. So Dewey ignored that policy. He actively recruited women, requiring tests, records, and, most questionably, photographs, saying that "you cannot polish a pumpkin." Seventeen of the first twenty students were women.

Exhausted by his constant manipulations and outraged by his latest, flagrant disregard for its authority, the Board of Columbia prepared to fire him, but, before it acted, he accepted a position as secretary of the New York State University and head of the New York State library, taking with him the School of Library Science.

From Albany—where he sometimes allowed young female students to stay at his house—he turned the New York State public system into a blockbuster. He sent traveling libraries everywhere, he set new standards for the professional development of librarians, and he saw his widely used classification system adopted throughout New York, the nation, and even in Europe.

Dewey remained a leader in the American Library Association until 1906, when he resigned under a cloud of innuendo about his continuing sexual harassment of female librarians. He and Annie moved to Lake Placid, where he founded the first Olympic Games in America.

Library Class, 1901 in Chautaugua

MEANWHILE ANDREW CARNEGIE

Between 1850 and 1896, the number of libraries—social, academic, professional, and public—was dwindling. In 1850, there were 10,000, and in 1896, there were 3,000. Long-term support for staff, space, and new books was hard to come by, and without public support, libraries struggled to survive.

Boston was one glorious exception. The city opened the first public library in the nation in 1848 to "advance intellectual and moral growth . . . and supply practical information." Soon it had some 12,000 books, and adults, including "oyster operators, cooks, errand girls, washerwomen, and shop girls" and students twelve to sixteen years old could check out one book a day, every day, free of charge. It was ahead of the curve.

But as immigration, industrialization, and urbanization changed American culture, people began to see libraries as a potentially stabilizing influence, and a vehicle for inculcating working people and newcomers with American values. Public support for libraries began to take hold.

Then along came Andrew Carnegie. Primarily self-educated, the hugely wealthy Scottish immigrant decided to dramatically increase his earlier gifts of library buildings. Starting in 1886, Carnegie offered to pay for the construction of a public library in any American town with more than 1,000 people if town leaders guaranteed space and annual support. With a massive financial carrot and smart strategic sense, Carnegie joined the movement to get local governments to support free public libraries.

THE SOURCE AND SHAPE
OF CARNEGIE'S PHILANTHROPY

Andrew Carnegie, the oldest of two boys of an impoverished family in Dunfermline, Scotland, immigrated to Alleghany, Pennsylvania, in 1848. He was thirteen years old. He immediately went to work, running back and forth in the aisles of a cotton mill, changing the bobbins. Affable and ambitious, he struck adults as capable and mature while sometimes alienating his peers. Within one year, he was delivering telegrams for $2.50 a week all around Pittsburgh. Trusted to connect businessmen with essential news from their families, customers across town, and their investors in New York, he earned more than his mother, an in-home shoemaker, and his father, a failed door-to-door salesman of handmade tablecloths.

In 1850, a local iron manufacturer, Colonel James Anderson, opened the library of 400 books in his house to the "working boys" of Pittsburgh. Every Saturday, he helped boys choose books. Soon overwhelmed by demand, Colonel Anderson donated the books to the city. But the semiprivate library struggled to survive, so the city leaders, unwilling to fund it, began to charge two dollars a year for anyone who was not a "working boy."

Young Andy Carnegie wrote the newspaper, arguing politely but firmly that, although he worked from an office, not a factory, he was still a "working boy." Suggesting that the generous patron intended to increase access to books, not limit it, he signed the letter "A Working Boy." The librarian took umbrage with some of Carnegie's claims, but within three days, Andy Carnegie was granted free library privileges.

"The windows were opened in the walls of my dungeon through which the light of knowledge streamed in . . ." he wrote in his 1902 *Autobiography*. Becoming a voracious reader, he landed an early blow for free public libraries.

Once Carnegie began to amass his enormous fortune from railroads, coal, and steel, he built libraries in towns that had personal and professional relevance, starting in his hometown in Scotland. Although later he rarely attended grand openings of Carnegie libraries, in 1881 he and his mother returned to Dunfremline, Scotland, the town they left, impoverished, under banners of welcome to open the library there. Eventually, Carnegie built libraries all around the world, including one in Fiji. Carnegie, unlike other magnates of the Gilded Age, promised to give all his money away. He outlined those intentions in a prenuptial agreement when he married his wife in 1887. Purportedly, his wife, Louise Whitfield, said she wished they had married when he was still struggling financially so that she could help him succeed. From all accounts, it appears that she shared his philanthropic instincts.

"The man who dies rich dies disgraced," he wrote in his essay "The Gospel of Wealth."

Carnegie believed that, like a musical virtuoso with a God-given talent, only a few men "possess the management and organizational skills to secure . . . enormous wealth." Writing as a realist, not a braggart, he believed that he was one of those few men, and he believed that great fortune—and his was purported to be the largest in the world—brought great obligation. He questioned how best to spend his massive wealth.

Huge inheritances leave "succeeding generations impaired" and postmortem distribution lacks vision, he posited. But disposing his fortune while he was alive meant he could address income inequality, not by dividing his wealth among individuals, but by supporting the common good. For Carnegie, it was not about charity to the unworthy—the poor who don't help themselves—but assistance to those who do. What better way than supporting public libraries,

Andrew Carnegie and His Favorite Magazine, 1911

an essential tool for self-improvement? Inspired by Colonel Anderson in Alleghany, Carnegie wrote that libraries "stimulate the best and the most aspiring poor of the community to further efforts for their own improvement."

Ever the savvy businessman, Carnegie knew that without steady support, libraries could not survive; therefore, his gifts could—in modern lingo—leverage public support and spur government action. He announced publicly his intention to build libraries with certain conditions—including public support—and he invited letters of request.

But violent riots at Carnegie's Homestead steel plant in July 1892 left many dead, a gritty town devastated, and Carnegie's reputation indelibly stained. A minister in Columbus, Ohio, labeled Carnegie's library offer "tainted money" and the sentiment spread. Eugene Debs, the fiery labor organizer, said libraries will be in "glorious abundance when capitalism is abolished and workingmen are no longer robbed by the philanthropic pirates of the Carnegie class." Mr. Dooley, Finley Peter Dunne's famous Chicago newspaper character, said, "The way to abolish poverty an' bust crime is to put up a brown stone buildin' in ivry town in the counthry with me name over it." Consequently, some communities said no thanks, but hundreds responded positively.

One such request came from a wheelchair-bound young man, Charles L. Thompson, in the town of Newnan, Georgia. He wheeled himself around town asking his neighbors what a library might offer them.

"Our city desires to provide better for the higher life of its people, and we would like very much to interest you in our place. We have read with increasing admiration of your splendid philanthropy . . . Would you be willing to offer the city $10,000 for the building if we agreed to furnish a suitable site and provide 10 percent of this sum annually for its maintenance?" The Mayor of Newnan added a postscript, saying he agreed, and two weeks later the town of Newnan received approval. Sadly, Thompson, the young proponent, contracted pneumonia and died within weeks of Carnegie's approval. The library opened in 1904 with tributes to young Thompson. Many years later—long after Carnegie's death too—the library was renovated. Newnan invited Louise Carnegie, who had never been invited to such an event, and she went, taking with her a portrait of her husband to hang above the fireplace in the library's reading room. It was the second of 24 public libraries and 5 academic libraries built with Carnegie money in Georgia alone.

Highly organized and centralized, Carnegie and his right-hand man, James Bertram, checked the accuracy of statements in each request, reviewed the plans, required formal approvals from the town councils, and then, if it all checked out, approved the projects, sending money as needed throughout construction.

Sometimes Carnegie and Bertram responded to requests with more money! Philadelphia, mindful of Carnegie's gift of branch libraries to New York, asked to build 30 branches for $30,000 each, but Carnegie said the figure was too low—the branches needed lecture rooms—and granted $50,000 for each.

What Carnegie did not do was involve himself in local politics. As long as the town gave the land and supported the annual costs at approximately $2 per person, he maintained a hands-off approach. He did not care what books it should buy or where the library should be built. In the South, this resulted in "colored branch libraries."

THOMAS FOUNTAIN BLUE AND THE "COLORED" BRANCH LIBRARIES OF LOUISVILLE

Louisville, Kentucky, was a mixed bag of ugly racism and hopeful opportunity for African-Americans. Schools were segregated, but the city of 224,000 had a high school for black students—a rarity in the South. Black teachers existed (something most places prohibited) and there were more than 100 of them, but they were paid far less than their white counterparts and were tested routinely for their loyalty to the status quo. Hospitals were segregated, but thirteen black doctors practiced in the city. African Americans could not, by law, work for the city government, but Louisville had an active Negro Businessmen's League. White churches sent black worshippers to rear pews, but more than fifty black ministers built strong congregations in black neighborhoods. The black elite owned nice houses, but most African Americans lived in decrepit houses in neighborhoods with unpaved roads and no sewers.

Thomas Fountain Blue, a black man, arrived in Louisville in 1899 at the age of 33. A college-educated, ordained minister, he ran the colored YMCA of Louisville. Providing "Christian uplift" to poor blacks, the Y offered classes, community rooms, a temporary shelter, and a small reading room since African Americans were not allowed in the public library.

In 1905, under pressure from black activists—particularly one fearless, biracial public school teacher, Albert Meyzeek—the city of Louisville opened a three-room "colored" library within its public system and hired the energetic Reverend Blue as its first librarian.

"All of us felt the sting of . . . segregation, but there were those among us who decided to make the most of it," said Rachel David Harris, the black children's librarian whom Blue hired. "The feeling

Thomas Blue and the staff of Western Branch,
Louisville Free Public Library.

of a perfect welcome, ownership and unqualified privilege are all
necessary to [library] patrons . . . and in the south can only be had
in separate branches."

The first book borrowed was Booker T. Washington's *Up
from Slavery*, and within three months, more than 4,000 people
visited the tiny library. The same year, Louisville applied for
Carnegie funds to build three new buildings, including two colored branches. Building colored libraries kept black people out of
the main library—an example of what one historian, George C.
Wright, labeled the "polite racism" of Louisville.

Deciding where a new public library should go was often
contentious, and Louisville and its black residents were no different. Should the first colored branch go where the better-ed-
ucated African Americans lived, or closer to the less advantaged

people? Despite an illiteracy rate of 27 percent among poor blacks in Louisville in 1908, the first colored library opened near where the educated, professional black people lived on the west side. The second opened a mile and a half away on the poorer, eastern side of town in 1914. Reverend Blue directed both.

Just two years after the first branch opened, Andrew Carnegie congratulated the head of the entire library system for "the splendid success of the library movement in Louisville and especially the department provided for colored people."

Reverend Blue, a creative manager, and his two assistants, both educated black women, built a network of programs and activities that eventually reached thousands of people throughout the entire county. Blue opened some seventy library delivery stations—mini-libraries—throughout the city where library patrons could borrow or return books without walking long distances or paying streetcar fares. The libraries buzzed with social, cultural, and intellectual life; in just one year alone, 498 meetings were held in the two "colored" libraries.

SEPARATE BUT TOGETHER

As far as we know, Dewey, Carnegie, and Blue never met, but their lives were inextricably linked. By the time Carnegie ended his library philanthropy in 1914, he had spent $41 million (more than $1 billion today), adding 1,406 free public libraries to America including 15 "colored branches" in the South. Many of those libraries added grandeur to towns and cities, with interiors that enhanced the library's many functions.

Inside, many libraries looked—and smelled—alike, thanks to the library-specific furniture and equipment Dewey sold in bulk. New York had 534 traveling libraries crisscrossing the state, and the Dewey Decimal system was firmly established. Thanks to Dewey's push for professionalism, many more librarians were trained, including many African American librarians in the southern "colored branches" who Reverend Blue invited and mentored in

Louisville. Library stacks were generally open, and more and more people saw government funding of libraries as appropriate, needed, and valuable.

WILLIAM MULHOLLAND:

Watering the Land of Eternal Sunshine

In early November 1913, on a typically perfect Southern California day, Los Angeles celebrated the opening of its first aqueduct, the lifeline to its future. Comparable in size and complexity only to the Panama Canal, the aqueduct stretched 233 miles underground, aboveground, and through mountains and blazing desert; it made the famous Roman Aqua Marcia look like "a section of a garden hose," writes author Les Standiford.

An estimated 40,000 people, almost one sixth of the entire population of the growing city of Los Angeles, gathered at the mouth of a tunnel in a rugged mountainside thirty miles from downtown. They arrived in buggies, on horseback, in special train cars, and 5,000 Model T Fords, fancifully decorated with pennants. They made their way through the Southern California canyons on newly scraped roads, dampened to keep the dust down.

The women wore long cotton dresses and wide-brimmed hats; men were in suits and caps, sailors in crisp uniforms, and Shriners wore their hats with red and gold tassels. Vendors hawked lemonade, sandwiches, and pie. Many people scrambled up the craggy, dusty hill to hover above the mouth of the tunnel; others waited several deep along the concrete channel for the big moment, eager to touch the water when it came. Thousands more waited in front of the dais. Everyone carried a drinking cup.

When the caravan of dignitaries arrived, the crowd broke into thunderous applause. Chief Engineer William Mulholland, "the sturdy man with the stern gaze," could barely make his way to the dais through the throngs of appreciative fans. Responsible for guiding this "glorious enterprise," as the Los Angeles Times called it, Mulholland—loved by many and hated by others—was sadly distracted that triumphant day; his wife and the mother of his children was hospitalized with the cancer that would kill her two years later.

But, as always, the aqueduct took precedence. After speeches and music, he stood to the roar of the crowd, thanked his colleagues, and then, with little fanfare, unfurled the flag that signaled the shooting of cannons and the turning of the valves. Water gushed from the tunnel and cascaded down the channel, as Mulholland said simply to the mayor, "There it is. Take it."

People cheered, threw their hats into the air and flowers into the water, and pushed their way to the canal to feel the cool water and dip their cups into it. Mulholland's granddaughter wrote that Mulholland saw a feathered Tyrolean hat blow into the torrents and heard the owner ponder, "I wonder how fast that water travels." A man of few, but exact words, Mulholland said, "You'll find your hat at the dam in seven minutes."

Tours of the brand-new nearby reservoir, a celebratory lunch, and an honorary dinner followed, and the next day marching bands and elaborate floats paraded downtown. Submarines, torpedo boats, and the battleship *South Dakota* noisily joined the exultations from the harbor.

William Mulholland, his engineers, and some 4,000 workers had finished the massive and complex six-year project ahead of schedule and under budget without a hint of

Jawbone Canyon, 1913

graft, but in a swirl of constant political controversy—controversy that continues to this day. But the aqueduct and its water would quench the thirst of millions, irrigate the arid land of the plain, line the pockets of a few, and allow the City of Angels to soar. Bill Mulholland, a man of unbound imagination and unfettered confidence, had done it.

MULHOLLAND'S BEGINNINGS

He was born in Belfast in 1855 to lower-middle-class Irish-Catholic parents. When Mulholland was five, the family moved to Dublin, a dark and depressing place after the Great Famine of the 1840s had devastated the Irish economy and spirit.

Mulholland's father, Hugh, was a guard with the British Royal Mail, protecting horse-drawn coaches from highway robbers that lurked between Derry and Dublin. The coveted job—not always given to Irish Catholics from the north—required a degree of literacy that many did not possess; a muscular toughness, given the dangers; and trust from the British, given the cargo. Hugh Mulholland passed those traits—intellect, ruggedness, and loyalty—onto his son. Young Willie, as he was then called, got his dry wit from his mother, Ellen, who died when he was only seven.

Home with his widowed father and three brothers must have been a sad and difficult place, and Mulholland rarely spoke about it, but his granddaughter and biographer, Catherine Mulholland, surmised that his later affinity for male friendship stemmed from those early days in a male-only home.

Hugh remarried three years later. He and his new wife had three children in rapid succession, and, although Jane was kind, she was distracted and busy with seven children at home. Rather than go home each afternoon after school, William and his brothers wandered the streets of Dublin with adolescent swagger. William argued with his gruff father; by the time he was fifteen, he had dropped out of school, not once but twice, and left Dublin for good, never returning to "that damned island of my childhood."

Enamored of the fully rigged ships that sailed out of Dublin under the protection of the British Navy, he joined the merchant marines and, over the next four years, crossed the Atlantic nine-teen times. He saw ports throughout North America and the West Indies, and mastered the complexities of wind and water. In June 1874, the six-foot tall, ramrod-straight, blue-eyed Mulholland left the merchant marines in New York and began four more years of exploration. He was nineteen years old.

He sailed the Great Lakes, cut white pine in Michigan for-ests, bounced through Ohio as an itinerant knife sharpener, and learned the retail business with an aunt and uncle in Pittsburgh. Somewhere along the way he read, as thousands of others did, Charles Nordhoff's *California: For Health, Pleasure and Residence: A Book for Travelers*, published in 1873.

". . . very few suspect that the Californians have the best of us and that, so far from living in a kind of rude exile, they enjoy, in fact, the finest climate, the most fertile soil, the loveliest skies, the mildest winters, the most healthful region, in the whole United States," wrote Nordhoff.

Mulholland later said he "had no peace" until he saw California, so with his brother, Hugh, he stowed away on a ship sailing from New York to California. Discovered, they were dropped ashore in Panama. They walked across the isthmus and found work on ships, first to Acapulco and then on to San Francisco. From there, with Nordhoff on his mind, he and Hugh rode horseback south through the San Joaquin Valley with the towering Sierra Nevada to the east and the coastal range to the west. In January 1877, they arrived in the town of Our Lady the Queen of Angels on the arid, coastal plain of Southern California.

Described by one settler as a "torpid, suppurating, stunted little slum," the pueblo had 9,000 people, mostly Mexican and Chinese laborers. "Unassimilated, unwelcome, and unprotected," as historian Robert Fogelson writes, they were marginalized and sometimes brutalized. On one horrific night, before Mulholland arrived, hundreds of white men attacked the Chinese section of town, smashing houses, beating people, and lynching twenty Chinese men.

Willie and Hugh did not linger, but immediately headed to Arizona to pan for gold and sail the Colorado River. If they had wanted, they could also have become mercenaries to fight Indians.

"There were a great many hostile Indians about . . . it was one of those cases where presence of mind was best secured by absence of body," quipped Mulholland many years later.

They went back to the pueblo in California, where William returned to water, albeit the small and unreliable Los Angeles River. He fell in love with "the beautiful, limpid little stream with willows on its banks . . . so attractive . . . that it became something about which my whole scheme of life was woven."

The river, which flowed south from the Santa Monica Mountains, was connected to the pueblo by one hand-dug channel from which nine three-foot-wide and one-foot-deep canals, called "zanjas," radiated. Women collected water from and washed clothes in them, men irrigated the fields with them, and Mulholland landed a job removing debris and dead animals from them. Paid $1.50 a day, he lived alone for two years in a tiny shack where he read all night. With broadening interests and a photographic memory, he studied everything from Shakespeare to civil engineering, geology to hydrology. Many years later, the brusque, ribald, and self-taught engineer stunned a friend's wife when he broke out in song from Gilbert and Sullivan.

LOS ANGELES AND THE POWER OF PROMOTION

As the rest of the population of the United States grew in number and shifted from east to west, Southern California remained relatively unknown—and misunderstood—among potential settlers. Most who went west, historian Charles Willard wrote, went for gold in northern California, never traveled south, and returned home empty-handed and disappointed.

But in 1876, when the Southern Pacific Railroad inaugurated the first train from San Francisco to Los Angeles and promoted the "sunlit skies of glory," invalids began to arrive for healing doses of the weather. Nevertheless, the permanent population did not grow substantially. Even with the sea, the sky, the sun, and the mountains, Los Angeles "found itself a merchant with a fine stock of goods on hand, but no customers," writes journalist Morris Rathbun. The Great Lakes, the Pacific Northwest, and other regions were attracting the entrepreneurial immigrants. "Their success was Southern California's failure," Robert Fogelson writes.

But ten years later, when the Atchison, Topeka, and Santa Fe railroad linked Los Angeles directly to the east through St. Louis and Omaha and dropped the ticket price from $125 to $1, radical transformation began.

"For a dollar, you could hop a train for Paradise," Les Standiford writes.

Although Los Angeles eventually epitomized growth through suburbanization, not urbanization, every growing city in America of any size at that time had a chamber of commerce or board of trade and Los Angeles was no different. Its historian, Charles Willard, argues that the LA Chamber was noticeably different than others in several key ways: Its membership was proportionately much larger for its size than other cities and far more diverse, including retailers and manufacturers, bankers and railroad owners, doctors and lawyers, ministers and professors. It had visionary leaders, who saw the long-term potential of the area and believed in the value to individual businesses of economic development for all. And it had Frank Wiggins.

A Quaker hardware salesman from Indiana, Wiggins went to Southern California in 1890 in poor health, prepared to die. However, his health improved, and he found his voice as the energetic head cheerleader of Los Angeles. He "never sleeps when it comes to keeping the universe informed about Los Angeles . . . people are lectured, pelted, beaten, and bruised with an avalanche of information," wrote journalist Frances Groff in 1910.

When his chamber colleagues wanted more experienced farmers, Wiggins aggressively recruited in the Midwest. He sent prefabricated and easily installed exhibits to state fairs and trade shows, and opened a promotional storefront in Chicago. He flooded the rail lines with 900 cars decorated with oranges and, understanding branding way ahead of his time, he slapped colorful Sunkist labels for the first time on every crate of Southern California oranges. He hung beguiling posters in small Iowa towns; soon a section of Los Angeles became known as Iowa-by-the-Sea. In Omaha, a town of 140,000, Wiggins dropped enough brochures for every man, woman, and child.

Want to turn those tourists into lifelong residents? Entice them with a permanent exhibit downtown with a Venetian bridge built from oranges, a circus elephant sculpted from Southern California walnuts, and cheerful dwarfs sitting atop a mammoth registry for visitors to sign. LA need a harbor? Annex San Pedro. Then send cruise ships to Hawaii and welcome the navy. Need more jobs? Promote clean air, weak labor unions, inexpensive land, and cheap electricity and convince Goodyear to come—followed soon by others. And what about the romance of LA's Spanish and Mexican past? Attract the earliest film studios with perfect weather and endless locations.

". . . 80 million people in the United States and they all want to come to Los Angeles," wrote Groff.

Between 1900 and 1910, Wiggins's first decade on the job, Los Angeles grew by 103 percent, compared to New York's 37 percent and Chicago's 54 percent. The following decade it grew by 212 percent, compared to New York's 39 percent and Chicago's 29 percent. During Wiggins's tenure, a whopping 60 percent of tourists to Los Angeles returned for good. Its population increased from 50,000 to 310,000, and estimates predicted 2 million within 20 years. Every house, business, and person needed water, and yet the area had little. William Mulholland said the only way to solve the long-term water supply problem was to kill Frank Wiggins.

THE TAKING OF OWENS VALLEY

The Paiute Indians' lives also revolved around water. For thousands of years, this small tribe lived peacefully in an isolated but dramatic sliver of land north of where the Mojave Desert and the

Sierra Nevada meet. Squeezed between the majestic, snow-capped Sierras on the west and the mineral-laden White-Inyo Mountains on the east, the 100-mile long Owens Valley, starting at a shallow and salty lake, depended almost entirely on the snowmelt from the Sierras. Living in twig huts, the Paiutes harvested pine nuts in winter and seeds and berries in the springtime, and they diverted water from the numerous mountain streams with simple dams and canals to cultivate fields below.

But then prospectors came—including Mark Twain—followed by cattle ranchers and farmers, who drove the Paiutes off their land and commandeered their irrigation system. And when William Mulholland and his former boss, Fred Eaton, arrived in the Owens Valley, everything changed forever for everyone.

A self-taught engineer, Fred Eaton, the privileged son of a prominent Southern California family, was elected mayor of Los Angeles in 1898 and was determined to wrestle control of LA's water from the private company that had held the license for many years. Contentious issues of access, availability, and fair prices dominated the struggle.

Mulholland, by then head of operations for the company, agreed with Eaton that water should be municipally owned—a highly controversial issue in those days, particularly if one worked, as Mulholland did, for the private water company. In 1902, when the license expired, Los Angeles regained control of its own water supply and the newly empowered Los Angeles Water Department hired Mulholland as its leader.

Never seeking wealth, only work he loved, Mulholland reveled in being the chief engineer for the city, building a new reservoir, laying new pipe and connections, and installing water meters to conserve water and reduce cost to consumers—all designed to address the growing need for water. But occasional droughts, including one in 1903–04, dramatically lowered the already inconsistent Los Angeles River, even as Wiggins pushed—and achieved—extraordinary growth. With each new business or new home (now with flush toilets and bathtubs more common), the need for water became urgent.

On top of that, a group of speculators from LA bought 16,000 acres in the San Fernando Valley, outside the city limits. They had no water either, but the court had ruled, after much dissension and debate, that the water from the old pueblo belonged to the city of Los Angeles—and only Los Angeles.

Fred Eaton owned land in the Owens Valley and had long believed it was the solution to LA's water problem. Never having been there, but well aware of the mountains and the desert, Mulholland was skeptical. Nevertheless, in 1904, Eaton and Mulholland piled onto a buckboard pulled by mules and loaded with beans and booze, and bounced 250 miles through the canyons and desert, past the 15-mile-long Owens Lake into the heart of the sparsely populated valley 4,000 feet above Los Angeles, with multiple streams pouring down the rugged walls of the Eastern Sierras. The potential dazzled Mulholland, a man of self-confidence and great imagination. He said he could build an aqueduct and use gravity to deliver the water 233 miles away. Unfazed by the scope of the project, Mulholland said, "The man who has made one brick can make two bricks. That is the bigness of this engineering problem. It is big, but it is simply big."

Mulholland did worry, however, that, if the plans became public, speculators would jack up the price of land. His eagerness to solve the water problem blinded him to the downside of secrecy and haunted him for the rest of his career. Eaton, on the other hand, wanted to make money.

With permission from Mulholland's board to use surplus funds from the water meters, Mulholland and Eaton began to buy land. They told local farmers and ranchers that Eaton wanted to increase his holdings. A few people in Owens Valley were suspicious and soon the ambitious scheme became public, causing consternation and seeding greed. A local banker said, "You have paid high prices not because you're dumb, but because you're smart. You're masquerading as investors and all you're going to do is invest in our ruin."

Los Angeles's desire for water was also up against the federal government. With its newly established Reclamation Service, it was looking to turn barren, federal land into productive agricultural land through large irrigation projects. Owens Valley with its primitive but existing irrigation system was one of its early targets of interest. The 500 or so farmers of the Owens Valley looked hopefully on the possibility.

The Reclamation Service hired as a consultant Joseph Lippincott, an engineer, to assess the project's feasibility. He began his study and, simultaneously, agreed to work as a paid consultant to Mulholland. Lippincott—and Mulholland—believed in Lippincott's professional integrity, but when Lippincott sided with Mulholland over the federal project, his obvious conflict was exposed and he was pilloried.

"We should have to call Mr. Lippincott, the villain, the character with the dark mien . . . and a hissing, snarling manner of speech," the local Owens Valley Chamber wrote.

Later Mulholland hired him, another questionable judgment call that fed the roiling controversy. Marc Reisner, an environmental historian, believes that Mulholland was a better engineer than politician, but one could also say that Mulholland just ignored perceptions and others' schemes when they stood in the way of his projects.

In 1906, President Roosevelt had to make a choice between the Reclamation Service and Los Angeles. Writing "aside from the opposition of a few settlers in Owens Valley whose interest is genuine, but whose interest must unfortunately be disregarded in view of the infinitely greater service to be served by putting water in Los Angeles," Roosevelt ordered the Reclamation Service to withdraw and granted Los Angeles the right to use federal lands to extract and deliver water to the city.

In his letter, Roosevelt added that he hoped LA would never sell the water to any other municipality or private entity—and it never did. However, after the aqueduct opened, the city annexed the San Fernando Valley, dramatically increasing the wealth of the powerful businessmen who had bought land there earlier—exposing their clear agenda and adding more fuel to the raging fire of controversy.

But first the aqueduct had to get built, and, to do so, the city needed money. Mulholland developed a preliminary plan and budget, and in June 1907, 24,000 voters of Los Angeles ignored the political and conspiratorial complexities and approved, ten to one, a $23 million bond issue to build an aqueduct that would bring 260 million gallons every day to Los Angeles—and, the city officials said, be sufficient for 25 years. It's hard to believe that if the voters had seen the route, they would have assumed such a financial burden, but their trust in Mulholland won the day. Now he had to do it.

PLANNING A BEHEMOTH

First he plotted the aqueduct's route from the mountain streams and valley springs south to the scorched Mojave Desert into red rock canyons and into foothills—places pummeled with sand, wind, snow, blazing heat, and frigid cold. Mulholland sent 200 engineers to the field to answer thousands of critical questions: How did the elevations change, and how did the soil and rock differ? Yes, gravity would pull the water, but how would the water get up, and which hills, before it went down them? Where would they need tunnels (eventually, 53 of them)? They staked out the aqueduct's final path, placing stakes every 50 feet along 233 miles.

To build the aqueduct, they needed 210,000 tons of material, but the closest train was 100 miles away in the town of Mojave. The iron would come from Pittsburgh and mule teams could haul it, but the mules would need to carry their own food and water, on round-trips, which would take days and days. So Mulholland negotiated a deal with Southern Pacific to build a rail line on land that cost them nothing and then haul the freight at a special rate. The rail line eventually paralleled the path of the aqueduct, but Mulholland needed roads—505 miles in total—to use before the railroad was completed and to connect the rail to the various worksites once the train was operational. Mules would be used initially and always on those connecting lines, so barns had to be built.

Mule Power at the Aque-duct, 1912

Where would they buy concrete for the conduit? They dug three limestone quarries in the mountains. They needed clay? Drain Owens Lake in the spring and dig enough clay from it each summer to last the year, and then build aerial cables to ferry the limestone and clay to the new concrete mill they built. What about the dredging machines? Owens Valley had no electricity. Construct two hydroelectric power plants and then lay 180 miles of conduit to deliver the electricity. String some 240 miles of telephone lines from the LA headquarters to sites along the way to ensure communications.

In 1907, the revenue from the bonds started to roll in; by the middle of 1908, most of the infrastructure was in place and construction could begin. Mulholland told his board that "the preliminary work has been appalling in its magnitude and expense," but lightning could not have moved any faster—and the good planning paid off at the end.

THEN BUILD

With bids from private contractors far higher than Mulholland's estimates—one even 100 percent higher—he decided to do all the work "in house." He needed engineers, supervisors, tunnelers, riveters, diggers, muckers, electricians, carpenters, clerks, mule drivers, blacksmiths, and shovel operators; and he needed as many as 4,000 at any one time. It is estimated that 100,000 men worked on the aqueduct over the five years.

The day laborers earned anywhere from $2 to $4 per day, and the more skilled workers, including engineers, earned anywhere from $70 to $800 per month. But they all had to work in isolated camps, sometimes in intense heat, for ten to twelve hours per day.

"Whistling Dick" was one of the workers. A master mule team driver, he came to the Owens Valley from Death Valley to drive 20-mule teams over rocky and uneven terrain, carrying 36-foot, 26-ton pipes to various sites. "The mountainsides echoed to Dick's commanding whistles and the crack of his black snake," described one colleague.

About two thirds of the unskilled day laborers were foreign-born immigrants, including Chinese, Mexicans, and southern Europeans. Many were transient, single men who often stayed for just one pay cycle, taking full advantage of the makeshift saloons that cropped up along the aqueduct's path.

"One crew drunk, one crew sobering up, and one crew working" was how one supervisor described his crews. Men drank on their breaks and brawled on payday; sometimes the fights were between various ethnic groups. Booze became a real problem, so Mulholland went to court to prohibit any bar within four miles of the aqueduct's path. In 1910, some thirty saloons closed.

The men all lived in work camps, spread 6 to 23 miles apart, each housing as many as 160 men in a few wooden houses and large sleeping tents, with a cook shanty, a mess hall, an office or two, sometimes a barn, always a machine shop, sometimes a clinic, and usually one shower.

Within one year, the teams had built fifty miles of aqueduct at half the projected cost. To maintain that impressive speed, Mulholland established a bonus system. The supervising engineers set ten-day completion projections for each section and, if the teams beat their own projection, each worker and staff engineers received a bonus, paid from the money saved. A riveter, for instance, who earned $3.50 a day, received 55 cents extra.

Mulholland experienced these conditions too. He often went to the field throughout the entire six years, eating in the mess halls and sleeping in the camps. One of Mulholland's daughters once said, "Oh, Father? You mean the man who occasionally comes to dinner?"

Invariably wearing work clothes, with a cigar in his mouth, Mulholland watched the men digging ditches, blasting rock, heaving pipes, or pouring concrete. Unpretentious, with a comfortable if taciturn camaraderie with his men, Mulholland once learned that a worker who had been stranded in a half-built tunnel was safe and jokingly asked if the man was paying for the hard-boiled eggs being pushed to him through an opening! At night in a camp, under gas lamps with the staff engineers, he'd pore over the huge blueprints that hung in each camp office. He earned the staff's respect—until food, layoffs, and the union converged.

Mulholland and his team ran the mess halls, but private contractors could buy food in open markets and benefit from seasonal cost differentials, so Mulholland solicited bids. D. J. "Joe" Desmond, a 33-year-old entrepreneur from Los Angeles, was awarded the contract. He had won plaudits for providing food free to relief workers after the 1906 San Francisco earthquake, and now he was delivering food to work crews building rail lines in Southern California.

For the aqueduct, he managed three slaughterhouses, canteens for the sale of personal items such as chewing tobacco and cigars, and 31 mess halls (in the camps and at sites) from where he and his team served three meals a day. The workers paid 25 cents a meal or $5 for the entire week.

Desmond started strong, serving varied and hearty meals with meat, vegetables, and pies, but he underestimated his costs and the challenges of such rough conditions. With workers coming and going, their numbers were variable, so purchasing was difficult, and without refrigeration, meat spoiled, perishables were impossible to keep, and bugs appeared in the bread. The men complained and fights broke out.

Then, in March 1910, the sale of the aqueduct's bonds slowed down. Faced with a cash flow problem, Mulholland delayed the construction of some sections, laying off some workers. Consequently, fewer men ate, further decreasing Desmond's revenues; in response, Desmond increased the cost of each meal to thirty cents. Mulholland refused to increase wages accordingly. The workers were furious—lousy food for more money.

Their fury encouraged the Western Federation of Miners, a union with extensive experience in the rough Colorado mines and elsewhere to organize the workers. The union aligned itself with the private and influential power companies, which had always coveted Owens Valley, and in the summer of 1910, 700 men walked off the job. Mulholland was irate.

The strike did not last long. In October, two unionists (not WFM members) detonated a bomb at the Los Angeles Times, destroying the building and killing 21 people. Union organizing came to an immediate halt. In addition, the City of Los Angles bought some of the outstanding bonds and work on the aqueduct started again. But Mulholland refused to grant wage increases to the strikers, hired more men, and gave the new hires transportation money, which the earlier hires had not received.

That autumn, a mayoral election in Los Angeles got ugly. Some wanted Mulholland to run; he, in his inimitable style, said, "I'd rather give birth to a porcupine backwards than become mayor of LA." The Socialist candidate, Job Harriman, pummeled Mulholland anyway, claiming the aqueduct was unnecessary, poorly managed, and designed to enrich a few. Harriman lost by thirty points, and a livid Mulholland demanded an investigation of Harriman's accusations. The subsequent investigation was politically fraught, with angry resignations and incriminations, but no graft was uncovered.

When the aqueduct officially opened on November 5, 1913—ahead of schedule and on budget—many considered Mulholland heroic, but others continued to regard him as duplicitous. Burt Heinley, one of Mulholland's senior staff people, wrote, "Whatever the outcome and whatever the reward, no municipality has ever waged a battle so remarkable in all its phases as this city by the Western sea."

TROUBLES AHEAD

The outcome was water—plenty of it—and more controversy. LA did not need all the water; in fact, they needed only a quarter of the water that flowed. And, sure enough, the real estate speculators—the original syndicate that had bought thousands of acres of undeveloped land in the San Fernando Valley—wanted the surplus. But so did other communities.

Local law forbade the selling of municipal water outside its boundaries, so the City of Los Angeles had to annex any community that wanted the surplus. The San Fernando Valley won, making those early speculators far richer and magnifying the claims that an elaborate ruse took money from taxpayers to enrich a few.

Still more controversy followed. Mulholland had said, "Whoever brings the water brings the people." But by the early 1920s, LA's population had reached about 600,000, far more than had been predicted, and the City needed more water—less than 10 years, not 25 years, after the aqueduct had been built.

In Owens Valley, the aqueduct had little impact on farming, most of which happened north of the diversion at Black Rock Springs near Lone Pine. In fact, pear and apple orchards had tripled in number and the population had increased to 7,000 people. But the valley experienced a long and devastating drought—the farms, ranches, and orchards north of the diversion suffered—just as LA began pumping ground water there to supplement the reduced snowmelt in the aqueduct. Rightfully scared, the farmers demanded assurances there would be enough water for them. The City's response was to start buying up more land with water rights.

Farmers were pitted against farmers. "Owens Valley is full of whisperings, mutterings and recriminations," said one visitor. And, as farmers sold or failed, the small towns of Owens Valley shrunk too, leaving local businesses and banks with fewer customers.

Owens Valley demanded $18 million for a wholesale buyout of all land, including reparations for local town businesses.

Mulholland reacted badly to the grumbling, likening the farmers' dissatisfaction to hoof-and-mouth disease, and threatening to hang troublemakers from trees "if orchards still existed in the Owens Valley." Mulholland vehemently opposed both the price tag and the compensation for businesses. The atmosphere became toxic.

In May 1924, a dynamite blast blew a huge hole in a section of the aqueduct, not far from Alabama Hills. None of the forty men involved were arrested. Over the next three years, blasts destroyed hundreds of feet of the aqueduct at various points. Los Angeles sent armed guards with "shoot to kill" orders. They patrolled the dirt roads and flooded areas with searchlights at night. In one notorious incident, armed rebels held off guards for 65 hours as the rebels opened valves and let the water run into the desert.

Sympathy for the protestors was widespread. Some newspapers sided with them, and the state legislature even censured Los Angeles. Will Rogers, the humorist with a populist streak, said bitterly, "Ten years ago, this was a wonderful valley . . . but LA had to have more water for the Chamber of Commerce to drink more toasts to its growth, more water to dilute its orange juice, and more water for the geraniums to delight the tourists while the giant cottonwoods here died."

In the summer of 1927, at the height of the violence, two brothers who owned the bank in Owens Valley and led the resistance were arrested and convicted of embezzlement and sent to prison. Without its now-disgraced leaders, the resistance collapsed. Los Angeles eventually bought 92 percent of the entire valley.

ST. FRANCIS DAM AND THE MISERY OF MULHOLLAND

During the violence in Owens Valley, Mulholland reassured the people of Los Angeles their water service would not be disrupted—in part, because he had built another storage reservoir. Opened in 1926, in a sparsely populated, mountainous area of the city between two hydroelectric powerhouses, the St. Francis Dam held 12 billion gallons of water behind a massive, 200-foot-high, 700-foot-wide concrete wall. It lasted only two years.

On March 12, 1928, Mulholland, concerned about repeated reports of cracks and leaks, inspected the dam and declared it safe. But at midnight that night, the dam broke, hurtling 1,000-ton blocks of concrete down the valley, unleashing 100-foot-high waves that tore a 2-mile-wide swath of destruction 54 miles long all the way to the ocean. It took just 70 minutes to empty the dam as hundreds of houses were destroyed and 450 people were killed. The St. Francis dam collapse was the worst civil engineering disaster in 20th-century America.

"His figure was bowed, his face lined with worry and suffering . . . Every Commissioner had the deepest sympathy for the man who has spent his life in the service of the people of Los Angeles," the *Los Angeles Times* noted.

Nine investigations followed, by the coroner, governor, city council, county supervisors, the American Society of Civil Engineers, and others. Each panel explored, one way or another, Mulholland's capacities and judgment. They probed the plan, the foundation, the structure, its design, its construction, the operations, and the warning signals. They questioned other Mulholland dams he had built, and they dragged his reputation through mud as deep as the St. Francis muck. Most of the panels concluded that the rock along the coastal range was too shattered and too soft to hold a concrete dam, which was built, they said, without enough review.

When asked who was responsible, Mulholland repeatedly said, "I alone am the man." His granddaughter Catherine Mulholland maintained in her biography of Mulholland that accepting responsibility did not equate to accepting blame, and that "he remained unconvinced that an ultimate explanation had been reached." But his resistance to the conclusions was not defiance, and William Mulholland resigned in November 1928. He was 72 years old. Mulholland was, as journalist Matt Blitz, writes, "the savior of Los Angeles until he wasn't."

Occasionally, his opinion would be sought, but he never worked again. He lived with his eldest daughter, Rose, in LA, and often retreated to land he had acquired in the San Fernando Valley over the course of several years. He saw his children and grandchildren but admitted that "his zest for life [was] gone."

On July 22, 1935, six months after a debilitating stroke robbed him of his mobility and his voice, William Mulholland, age 78, died. Flags were lowered to half-mast, and his body lay in state in city hall. During a private funeral, the water to Los Angeles was stopped for a minute as silence swept over men and machines at work on the Colorado River Aqueduct—a 242-mile aqueduct that Mulholland had begun to plan in 1923, to bring yet more water to the City of the Angels.

DR. CHARLIE MAYO:
Cows, Pigs, and Public Health

In 1912, a steady stream of people (some estimates say as many as 15,000) climbed off the train in the small town of Rochester in southeastern Minnesota, seeking medical care. A typical Midwestern town with four-story brick buildings on its one paved street, one railroad line that enriched it, and churches of various denominations that defined it, this small town of 8,000 people, surrounded by corn and wheat fields, was known, paradoxically, around the world for its unique, world-class hospital.

But that same year, scarlet fever (a scourge that sometimes killed 30 percent of all its victims) also came to Rochester. With the telltale sign of a red rash spreading over rough skin, the patients, including many small children, also suffered brutal headaches and convulsive vomiting. The first 29 cases in Rochester were reported in the newspapers, but then the elected officials and the editors, fearful of causing more panic and hurting Rochester economically, went quiet and let the epidemic rage on.

One evening, Dr. Charlie Mayo, one of the town's two celebrated doctors, joined others and descended on a regular meeting of the local aldermen, demanding immediate action to stop the epidemic. The grossly underpaid, part-time public health officer whined, "Every time I try to do something, people protest."

"Then give me the job," Dr. Charlie snapped uncharacteristically, "they won't dare get me fired." Then, exhausted, he went home to his family, including his fifteen-year-old daughter Dorothy, who was permanently brain damaged from scarlet fever she had contracted a decade earlier.

At 1:30 a.m., Charlie Mayo awoke to three council members banging on the front door of his spacious, stucco house four miles outside of town. The public health officer had resigned, and the council members begged Dr. Charlie to take the job. Wearing only pajamas and a robe, Dr. Charlie, the small-town doctor with world-wide fame, was sworn in as director of public health for Rochester.

Public health was changing as science progressed and government's role grew. Minnesota was one of the leaders. A visionary head of its state board of health kept detailed records of climate, environmental conditions, and population shifts to track; New York City and Massachusetts laboratories were doing the same; and Dr. Walter Reed had discovered that mosquitoes carried yellow fever, and deaths plummeted. Public health—if done right—could control as well as prevent disease and prolong life. Dr. Charlie knew that.

He immediately quarantined any home with scarlet fever, halting the epidemic in its flight, and announced his intention to put public health in Rochester on a "scientific and business-like track," even as he continued to manage, with his brother, what would become known globally as the Mayo Clinic. A local public servant extraordinaire, he took no salary.

THE MAYO FAMILY

Born four years apart, William James (in 1861) and Charles Horace (in 1865) were two of five children born to William Worrall Mayo and Louise Wright. Two of their siblings died young—not uncommon when as many as one in five American children died in infancy. Another sister died in her twenties.

Their British-born father studied chemistry and medicine in Manchester as well as in London and Glasgow, two centers of medical advances and serious inquiry. But, as his grandson later wrote, "that strange, ferocious, striving and restless Grandfather of mine," William Worrall Mayo, left his studies before receiving his medical license and came to America in 1845.

A nomad by nature, he eventually went west and studied medicine in Indiana, which had one of the first microscopes in the country. He met his future wife, Louise Wright, an independent young woman, who had traveled alone at eighteen from upstate New York on canal boats and in covered wagons to Indiana. Tired of the malaria that plagued that low-lying state, Mayo headed north, drawn by the news of a healthy Minnesota. Louise later joined him, starting a millinery business as William worked as a ferryboat operator, a rural vet, a small-town pharmacist, and an itinerant family physician—sometimes all at once, often leaving Louise alone.

"I think Dr. Mayo, my husband, was the greatest man—the most useful man—I ever knew . . . the secret of his usefulness was that he never looked backward . . . [he] thought nothing about the past, very little about the present, but always about the future," Louise told a reporter in 1914 at age 88.

After several moves, in 1863 they settled in Rochester when he became the examining physician for volunteers to the Union Army from southern Minnesota. They never moved again. Dr. Mayo opened a medical practice and dove into civic affairs. Over time, even as he continued his medical work, he spearheaded the opening of a new high school and public library, and served as mayor and a state legislator.

His sons inherited his sense of civic responsibility, if not his love of politics. The boys grew up in Rochester, inseparable but different. Will was tall and blond, quiet, and formal; Charlie was short and dark-haired, gregarious, and rumpled. Will was articulate; Charlie mumbled.

"We all loved Charlie; he was easy and approachable, so democratic, but Dr. Will scared us," a nurse once said.

The Mayo home library was large, an intellectual and unfettered playground for their sons, who attended local schools, taking rigorous courses, including Latin and German, although neither ever excelled as a scholar. At home, they studied chemistry and physics with their father, and botany and astronomy with their mother.

"The biggest thing Will and I ever did," Dr. Charlie once said, "was to pick our mother and father."

Without any domestic help in the house, the boys sawed wood, helped with laundry, groomed their horse and cow, fed the chickens, and, starting as young children, assisted their father on house calls and in his office. They studied the skeleton of Cut Nose, a Sioux Indian executed along with 38 other Indians after an infamous uprising in 1862 in New Ulm, Minnesota. Dr. Mayo watched the hangings, and then took the corpse—not an uncommon practice at that time among doctors who had little, if any, hands-on clinical experience. He dissected and studied him, and then hung his skeleton in his office.

In the same spirit of inquiry, Dr. Mayo often performed autopsies in his office to check his diagnosis of a dead patient against reality. The boys watched as he dissected corpses, Charlie once holding on tight to the body's hair lest he fall off the table.

"We were reared in medicine as a farmer boy is reared in farming," Dr. Will explained.

OUT OF DISASTER COMES A HOSPITAL

One hot and humid August evening in 1883, when Will, age 22, was home from the University of Michigan Medical School, the brothers headed in the family's buggy to a local slaughterhouse to pick up a sheep's head on which they wanted to practice eye surgery. From sudden dark skies, a tornado, "like a great coiling serpent, darting out a thousand tongues of lightning," smashed into Rochester.

"Buildings were swept from existence. Trees were torn out and stripped of their leaves, timbers driven into the ground . . . the earth strewn with (dead) horses, cattle and debris," described the local newspaper the following day. Along with local Catholic nuns, the three Mayos cared for the wounded in makeshift clinics, and from the nightmare of a tornado the dream for a hospital was born.

Hospitals, particularly out west, were "pest holes of gangrene and death," writes one historian. If someone had to go to a hospital—and it was usually the poor who did so—their doctors were invariably poorly prepared without diagnostic tools and little if any medicine available. Surgery was the only option. A woman wide awake, tied to an unsanitary operating table, feeling "the dreadful steel plunge into [her] breast," or the Civil War soldier, biting a bullet, watching his leg sawed off, are vivid images of excruciating pain. And with infections rampant, only about 20 percent of surgical patients survived. Hospitals were "gateways to death."

But in October 1889, the Catholic nuns of Rochester and "old" Dr. Mayo opened a three-story hospital on nine acres of land, donated by Mayo, on a dirt road outside of Rochester. With 45 beds, it was the only hospital in southern Minnesota and the Dakota Territories, and was open to all despite one's ability to pay or one's religion. Always mechanical, Charlie designed the operating room with skylights and a table with special troughs to drain the blood, and hot water spigots for sterilization.

Charlie had graduated the year before from the Northwestern School of Medicine, where he benefited, as his father knew he would, from clinical work and new thinking. (Two decades later, an influential report assessed the state of medical education in America and recommended that 120 of the existing 150 medical schools be closed. The universities of Michigan, Minnesota, and Northwestern all passed.)

Dr. Charlie, then 23 years old, performed the first operation at the new hospital: the removal of a cancerous tumor from a patient's eye. Dr. Will assisted and their father, Old Doctor Mayo, administered chloroform.

By 1905, the hospital had 175 beds and the Mayo brothers were each performing as many as 3,000 operations a year with the highest survival rates of any hospital in America. People from all around the nation sought their help and doctors from all over the world came to observe them.

In one story, a Southern gentleman, needing abdominal surgery, traveled to New Orleans, then Memphis, and then Cincinnati, seeking out their respective specialists, but all three were sick and out of town. So, frustrated, he traveled to Rochester, and there discovered that all three doctors were patients at "the clinic in the cornfield," all because of one resourceful doctor and his two remarkable sons.

PUBLIC HEALTH IN RURAL AMERICA

Between 1900 and 1910, the population of America soared from 75 million to 92 million people. The explosion fueled a massive increase in demand for food, and the Golden Age of Agriculture began. Farmers in southern Minnesota added hogs, chickens, and cows to their "pioneer wheat farms," raising them primarily for their own use and enjoying the extra income they brought in—a fattened pig sold to the local butcher, fresh milk peddled to neighbors or distributors, eggs bartered for cloth, butter sold for a few cents. Soon Minnesota was one of the four top dairy states in the nation and had cornered the market for butter. With trains and a growing number of cars and paved roads, distribution of food to cities became easier and the countryside and the cities became inextricably linked.

In 1908, President Theodore Roosevelt's National Commission on Country Life released the first-ever report on rural America. "The strengthening of country life is the strengthening of the whole nation . . . The city dweller in the long run has only less concern than the country dweller in how the country dweller fares," it said.

Although health was better in rural areas than in cities where contagion spread quickly through congested conditions, the report stated bluntly that the health in rural America was in "urgent need of betterment."

Indeed. When Charlie became director of public health, he and Will, with their own money (the brothers shared a bank account their entire lives), hired a full-time physician with experience in public health to manage the day-to-day activities of the office. Charlie supervised him. One month, the doctor found 54 cases of smallpox, tuberculosis, scarlet fever, diphtheria, chicken pox, weak eyes, hearing problems, goiters, and conjunctivitis in the 765 children he examined. That was typical.

But a relatively new and related problem was also emerging: contaminated food. Consumers complained about flyspecks in butter, rats in meat, milk cut with chalk, murky ice, and rotten vegetables. Old Doctor Mayo found sand in sugar and publicly denounced such contamination, magnifying the concerns of Dr. Charles Hewitt of Red Wing, Minnesota.

Hewitt was the first secretary of the state board of health—one of the earliest such boards in the nation. He pushed sewage reforms such as separating wells from barns, outhouses, and farm kitchens; he established controversial but effective smallpox vaccination stations; and he embraced the new science of bacteriology, having once studied with Louis Pasteur in Paris. But milk, an essential but dangerous component of the American diet, was particularly problematic and became a heated and complicated political and medical problem. Deluged with complaints, particularly in the cities, Hewitt tried to convince local health officials to enforce standards of cleanliness, with decidedly mixed results.

In 1911, the state of Minnesota (with funds from women's groups) hired Caroline Bartlett Crane, "America's public housekeeper," to assess its health and sanitation. A former farmer, newspaper reporter, and Unitarian minister, Crane had stunned Michigan when she published a detailed description of the sorry state of its health conditions. Hired to do the same for Minnesota, she visited and reported on seventeen different places, writing that the "dark, dirty and most unsanitary dairies were in Rochester."

The following year, Dr. Milton Rosenau, a researcher and health official in Washington, DC who once lectured at Northwestern University, argued in his seminal work, *The Milk Question*, that "milk [was] the key to public health . . . and the weakest link in the sanitary health chain is the country health officer—if the city must depend upon the country health officer for the purity of its milk supply it is sadly handicapped." That year, Dr. Charlie became director of public health and made clean and pasteurized milk his signature issue.

GETTING CLEAN AND PASTEURIZED MILK

Cows lived in filthy barnyards, often deep in excrement, with pigs, chickens, and horses. The barns rarely had light, ventilation, or drainage. Cows were rarely washed and often had dung on their udders that fell into buckets or onto the fingers of the farmer, too few of whom washed their hands before milking. Most insidious, cows carried invisible diseases and passed them along to humans— tuberculosis, diphtheria, typhoid, and scarlet fever. Children were particularly vulnerable. Rosenau wrote that 2 million babies died before their first birthday between 1900 and 1910, and some 85 percent of those were not breast-fed.

"Nature never intended for milk of one animal to be used by the young of another," he wrote.

And yet milk had become a powerful force in the cultural, sociologic, and economic life of America. Some 23 million cows produced 10 billion gallons of milk annually in a business that had grown to $850 million a year nationally. Cows' milk was here to stay, so it had better be good.

National dairy conferences promulgated best practices; thanks to a wealthy philanthropist, New York City was breaking new ground; a well-respected doctor and researcher in the east published a widely circulated monthly bulletin, "Clean Milk"; and new equipment, such as milk cans with lids and milking machines, was available in the marketplace. Even with all those efforts, however, only 1 percent of the nation's milk was considered clean in 1912.

Dr. Charlie Mayo had seen this both at his practice and in the countryside, where he lived with his wife, Edith Graham, who was born one of thirteen children and had been a nurse before her marriage; and their eight children, six of whom were biological, one adopted, and one a foster child, on an estate they named Mayowood. Charlie designed the surprisingly cozy 38-room house, built around a large, old oak tree and filled with music from an Aeolian pipe organ. The estate eventually covered some 3,300 acres, with eight separate working farms.

Dr. Charlie said, laughingly, that a farmer earned his money on his farm and spent it in town, and an "agriculturalist" made his money in town and spent it on the farm. Edith often teased him about "the geese that flew away, the cows that died, and the chickens that didn't lay eggs," but it was only a joke. Charlie knew farming and knew how dirty farms caused disease. As director of public health, he proposed that Rochester mandate sanitation inspections of dairy farms and annual testing of cows for tuberculosis.

The farmers balked. Clean dairies required new space, new equipment, and new routines. They'd never "milk" a penny from more expensive dairy farms, they insisted. So Dr. Charlie turned Mayowood into a demonstration farm to prove a farmer could run a clean dairy and still make money.

With a spotless barn, sanitary utensils, milk cans with covers, milk cooled in ice, and cows tested for tuberculosis, Mayowood sold two different grades of milk: one "best for babies" from Holstein cows at twelve cents per quart, and the other Deluxe Golden from Guernsey cows at fourteen cents per quart—both sold in glass bottles with tops "specially protected by purity wrappers."

"Milk has never been so low in price or as high in quality," the Mayowood farm advertised; it made money and Dr. Charlie proved his point. In 1917, the Rochester council passed a clean milk bill, an important first step, but clean milk is not necessarily good milk.

THE MILK DEBATE

In the 1860s, Louis Pasteur, with his famous wine experiments, discovered bacteria and proved that heat can stop spoilage. But many doctors and scientists, believing that putrid air carried diseases, remained skeptical about germ theory, and the push for pasteurization—the heating and cooling of milk to stop the growth of bacteria that lurked in milk—became controversial.

Nathan Straus churned that debate. A German Jew who immigrated to America in 1854 with his parents as a six-year-old boy, Straus made a fortune owning Abraham and Straus and Macy's, two of the earliest and most successful department stores in America.

Uncomfortable with his wealth and encouraged by his wife, in 1893 Straus began to distribute pasteurized milk from his own plant to poor children in New York City. He wanted to end "the annual slaughter of innocents." He kept meticulous notes and, within four years, 20,000 children received his pasteurized milk regularly and only six died; 24 percent of all infants had died the year he began. He then wrote every mayor of every town and city in America, urging them to act.

"If one function of government is to control disease why not prevent it, too?" he wrote. "I was met with incredulity or with derision or with open and bitter attack."

Straus and his generosity (he eventually distributed 3–4 million bottles each year in 36 cities) continued to reduce deaths dramatically, but the arguments against pasteurization remained loud and strong. Opponents said that certifiably clean milk was good enough; pasteurization was not perfect and sometimes hid dirt, they said; pasteurization killed the nutritional value of milk and changed the taste, others said. But the main obstacles were farmers and scientists themselves.

The dairy farmers, facing an ever-changing and ever-more-layered distribution landscape, feared the economic impact on them. Commercial pasteurization—making the process cheaper by handling bulk—began at the end of the century. Pasteurization plants sprung up, selling their service to dairy farmers for a fee and marketing safe milk to the consumers at a cost. Consolidation of dairy farms followed, and small farmers felt threatened.

"[T]he farmer will have nothing to show for he cannot afford to pasteurize his milk," argued one Minnesota legislator sympathetic to the small guys. "This would result in large centralizers doing most of the business . . ."

The arguments raged. When strained milk leaves a clean barn, or even a pasteurization plant, no controls exist on the handling of the milk, they said. Why should the farmers and not the distributors shoulder the burden? Cows in Rochester are already tested for tuberculosis, and a cow can be tested annually and still come down with TB before the next test, they argued. Anyway, one sick cow can start an epidemic like scarlet fever that affects many people. Look what happened to Dorothy Mayo.

Melanie Du Puis, a historian, writes that the milk debate also reflected a growing divide between the city and the country. In the past, farmers were prototypical Americans, independent and self-reliant, but attitudes were shifting, exacerbated in part by adulterated and higher-priced food in the cities. Some city people began to see country people as ignorant and uncouth, or, as David Danbom, another American historian, writes, farmers came "to symbolize the worst of selfish, destructive and unrestrained individualism."

Another obstacle to pasteurization was that scientists did not agree on what constituted effective pasteurization. They debated ideal temperatures, ranging from 50 degrees centigrade to 100 degrees, and they disagreed how long milk should be heated, from one minute to six hours. But then Rosenau, supported by President Roosevelt, proved that milk heated to at least 142 degrees Fahrenheit for 30 minutes and then immediately cooled to 50 degrees or lower was ideal.

With that knowledge, the state of Minnesota promulgated standards for pasteurization, but without local support and local enforcement, pure milk was impossible to achieve.

President Franklin D. Roosevelt with Charlie and Will Mayo

"I do not contend that pasteurization will make unclean milk clean. I do contend, however, that pasteurization will and does make unsafe milk safe," wrote Dr. Charlie. He pushed for mandated pasteurization, copying tiny Winona, Minnesota, the only town in the state to have done so.

Farmers were furious. To satisfy earlier demands for clean milk, many had spent money to retrofit their barns, move outhouses, take better care of their cows, and keep dirt, dust, and dung out of milk cans. Mandatory pasteurization would mean new equipment to "cook and cool" the milk or paying a commercial plant to do it for them. Why, there was even talk about requiring glass milk bottles!

"Dr. Mayo wants to make Rochester dairy farms observe rules almost as strict as those in force in his own operating room. He wants the milkmen to wash their hands with antiseptic soap . . . to wear spotless clothing, handle the milk in specially equipped cooling rooms, and pasteurize every drop of it," wrote one Twin Cities newspaper.

But Dr. Charlie persisted. As he rewrote the original clean milk law, small farmers, distributors, and their supporters organized. The night the elected officials debated the final bill in August 1925, many of the opponents, including one woman, appeared at city hall. The national and global respect and fame Dr. Charlie enjoyed did not protect him from the hostility of the opposition. Furious with the very suggestion of a pasteurization mandate and worried about their own existence, they demanded that the aldermen defeat the bill.

Dr. Charlie fought back, first with science and reason and later with an impassioned plea about the common good, saying the aldermen should protect the public, not the profits of an industry in flux. Late that night, the bill passed by just one vote. Pleased, Dr. Charlie Mayo then surprised everyone and offered the woman, who had protested, the position of dairy inspector. After years of close study, incremental steps, and fierce advocacy, Rochester got pasteurized milk. The state of Minnesota did not mandate pasteurization until 1948.

PIGS, GARBAGE, AND A CLEVER RESPONSE

America at the turn of the century was not yet drowning in plastic, paper, or aluminum. People used, and reused, glass or tin containers; if they bought meat and vegetables at the store instead of growing their own, the food came wrapped in burnable brown paper or reusable burlap bags. People canned their extra fruit and vegetables and sprinkled coffee grinds and eggshells in their gardens. Everyone in small towns and farms had a "burn barrel" out back, and anything combustible went into it or the kitchen stove. But times were changing, and signs pointed to more and more waste disposed of in more systematic ways.

George Waring in New York had organized large-scale and equitable garbage collection, and one study by the Massachusetts Institute of Technology estimated that by 1902 more than 160 cities and towns around America had some basic solid waste collection. They burned the waste or, more often, dumped it, as land was plentiful and incinerators were filthy. But not Rochester.

In 1912, only twenty houses and the hospital had private, weekly pickups, for which they paid one dollar a week. Most Rochester families and businesses threw their garbage into backyards or onto streets or dumped it in the river. Some waste was hauled to the town dump, where scavengers hunted items or men sometimes gathered to shoot rats; occasionally, the waste was burned.

Some towns had piggeries and fed food waste to the hogs. But again, not Rochester. So Dr. Charlie worried about pigs too! He convinced the Council to support the collection of food waste three times a week, and then he proceeded to demonstrate that the effort could pay for itself. Like with his demonstration dairy farm, he bought thirty acres of land and purebred hogs, the equipment necessary to sort garbage, and started feeding the garbage to the pigs.

Butchers refused to buy the fattened hogs until they saw the operation—then they became converts. Worried about the competition, however, pig farmers argued that Rochester did not have the authority to collect the waste. When they learned they could not win that argument, they went to court, claiming the piggery was, ironically, a health hazard. But Dr. Charlie persisted and won. Within several years, Rochester Hog Farm repaid the initial investment of $17,000 and made $7,000 in profits. Dr. Charlie then gave the land, the hogs, the equipment, and the truck to the town with the understanding that all future profits support public health initiatives.

HIS FINAL DAYS

The Mayo Clinic grew and grew with new doctors, new divisions, and new buildings. Each year, both brothers performed hundreds of operations, Dr. Will specializing in abdominal surgery and Dr. Charlie in ear, nose, and throat operations. They worked every morning and then in the afternoons participated in the collaborative consultations with individual patients that made the clinic unique and admired. They both traveled, Dr. Will in the autumns and Dr. Charlie in the spring, visiting hospitals and doctors throughout the world. (Old Doctor Mayo, a veritable rolling stone, took his last trip to Asia in 1907 at age 88.)

In 1917, the Mayo brothers did something remarkable: They dissolved the partnership that was making them and their partners rich, put everyone on salary (not profit sharing), and directed all profits back into the newly formed not-for-profit institution, endowed and enriched forever.

In 1924, some Democrats tried to recruit Charlie as the Democratic nominee for president, predicting that Charlie's fame, folksy ways, and moderate positions might give Republican Calvin Coolidge a run for his political money. Hungry for an "honest surgeon who could cut graft out of Washington, DC," both Republican and Democrats in Minnesota loved the idea of a favorite son candidate. Dr. Charlie remained noncommittal for a while—perhaps flattered by the suggestion—but not interested in elective office, he finally said he was busy enough at work.

In 1927, Dr. Charlie resigned as director of public health, and two years later (two years after Will) he retired from medicine too. The brothers both stepped down from the Board of Governors of the clinic, wanting the public to gain confidence in the other doctors and the institution itself. No Mayo relative or descendent was promised a place at the clinic.

An avid horticulturalist, Dr. Charlie tended some forty varieties of chrysanthemums in greenhouses he built in fields below the main house, and spent his winters in Tucson, Arizona, where he and Edith built a house right next door to Will and his wife, Hattie. When the brothers received the first report from the clinic after their departure from the board, Charlie said, "Well, well, this is quite a comedown for us, Will. They're doing better now we're away than when we were there."

In the spring of 1939, Charlie was in Chicago when he was rushed to the hospital. Diagnosed with pneumonia (in the days before antibiotics), Dr. Charlie Mayo died, surrounded by his large and loving family, but not his beloved brother, who was recovering from stomach cancer. It was May 26, 1939. Charlie was 73 years old. Headlines blasted the sad news nationwide and 10,000 people filed past his coffin as he lay in state back at the clinic. Two months later, Dr. Will died.

SENATOR JAMES MCMILLAN:

The Quiet Power Behind
Modern Urban Planning

On a pleasant summer day in August 1902, Senator James McMillan played with his grandson and chatted with his wife at their gracious summer home on the coast of Massachusetts. He was taking it easy after two rough years—a son, a grandson, and his brother had all died, and the former governor of Michigan, an early Progressive and a mean-spirited demagogue, had relentlessly attacked him. He needed a quiet summer, and so it was even more shocking—and sad—when after dinner, James McMillan suffered a massive heart attack and died. He was 64 years old.

A private train carried his body back to Detroit, where his family held a funeral in their elegant house. State offices closed, flags hung at half-mast, factories throughout the city observed a moment of silence, flower shops from Cincinnati to Detroit sold out his favorite rose, and almost 7,000 people turned out to watch his burial at the cemetery. Later, US senators and congressmen, forty in all, stood on the floor of the Senate one by one to pay tribute to their colleague, who had rarely spoken in that forum but commanded rapt attention whenever he did.

"He was not an orator; he was not a genius; he laid no claim to brilliance, but he was in the best sense a man who accomplished things and whose every act enriched his fellow-man," stated Senator Orville Platt from Connecticut.

McMillan had enjoyed huge financial and political success,

contributed generously to the civic and cultural life of Detroit, controlled the Republican Party in Michigan, benefited from various tax breaks, and was elected unanimously by both political parties as senator in 1888.

His greatest legacy, even if now unknown, came when President McKinley asked Senator McMillan to handle the political and logistical complexities surrounding the capitol's centennial celebration. With shrewd political instincts, McMillan carved a path through the thicket of competing ideas and power grabs. He managed the process, diffused objections, sold the idea, and ensured the vision's sustainability—key components to its long-term success.

Known as the McMillan Plan of 1901–1902, it was the first permanent expression of the City Beautiful Movement and the kickstart to modern urban planning. The US Commission of Fine Arts reported that the "consummate artistry and professionalism of the designers . . . and their enduring commitment to implementation by the tactical shrewdness of their backers and plain good luck in negotiating Washington politics with mounting public success brought success."

James McMillan never lived to see the plan's full expression, but within seven years, more than 35 American cities and towns had developed comprehensive plans with sensible street arrangements, often a central railroad station, elegant civic buildings grouped together, unified park systems, and stylish streetscapes—and soon, of course, Washington, DC was well on its way to becoming, arguably, one of the most beautiful cities in the world.

McMILLAN'S YEARS IN DETROIT

Seventeen years old, deliberative and determined, practical and patient, James McMillan arrived alone in Detroit in 1855. He had finished a prestigious grammar school in his hometown of Hamilton, Ontario, where he was the oldest of eight children, born to Scottish immigrants on May 12, 1838. Not particularly academic, he was uninterested in college, but wanted to go straight into business, like his father, who was a founder of the Canadian Great Western Railroad.

Situated on a narrow river, Detroit, with 40,000 people, served as the commercial hub for surrounding farms. James landed a job at a local hardware store, but within two years—thanks to his father's help—he became the purchasing agent at the Detroit & Milwaukee Railroad, where he made his first mark. With a modest style, he managed the finances, purchased the supplies, and supervised the construction of a railroad extension between freight trains and steamships. He saw how local transportation was key to commerce and growth and, gifted with the power of foresight, he saw how the Detroit River could become the connector to the Great Lakes. That insight was the source of his future fortune and influence—and he was still a teenager!

When federal plans for a transcontinental railroad became a reality, lucrative times followed. James McMillan and his friend John Newberry assumed control of the Michigan Car Company that produced freight cars. Between the building of the continental railroad and the raging of the Civil War, they sold every train car they manufactured. Soon they purchased the Detroit Wheel Company, producing rather than purchasing wheels for their trains. McMillan understood that infrastructure, fueled by new innovations and technologies, drives economic growth, and in those early days of the American industrial revolution and nascent city governments, private industry built, owned, and operated urban infrastructure. In another big play, McMillan and Newberry took the state's offer of 1.3 million acres of resalable land and built a railroad to the Upper Peninsula of Michigan, merging it with another railroad and opening the Upper Peninsula to the East Coast.

Soon McMillan had financial interests in iron furnaces, pipes, shipbuilding, steam engines, steamships, and dry docks—all in Detroit. He then moved into the streetcar business, utilities, and telephones; he became the first president of the Michigan Telephone Company, introducing private phone numbers to Detroit residents.

"His business interests read like a fairy tale," said one colleague. By 1870, the number of industrial jobs in Detroit had climbed from

2,000 to 10,000, many of them due to McMillan's investments and ingenuity. Cited by historian Geoffrey Drutchas as the man "with the Midas touch," McMillan was president of twelve different Detroit-based companies and an investor in many more. He was a millionaire by 35.

"He was more than a captain of industry, he was a creator of industry and an organizer of industry—his activities an industrial endless chain," reported the *Detroit Free Press*. He transformed Detroit into a powerful industrial city.

HOME LIFE AND CIVIC INVOLVEMENT

McMillan and his wife, Mary Wetmore, the daughter of another successful Detroit businessman, raised six children, two of whom died as young adults. A close family, they built a large four-story house on East Jefferson Avenue, filled with art and McMillan's collection of Napoleon Bonaparte ephemera, a telling hobby for a calm yet driven man. They spent their weekends on Grosse Pointe, a peninsula north of Detroit (now an upscale suburb), which they reached on a private steam yacht moored off Jefferson Avenue. McMillan was charitable there, supporting his church and helping to build a golf course and racetrack. In Detroit, he was equally charitable, giving money to individuals in need and to institutions of cultural and educational value, including the University of Michigan, the Detroit Institute of the Arts, and a college for African-American women in Texas.

As cities grew into sprawling, ugly places, covered in smoke and soot, industrialists like McMillan became interested in their beautification. Pleasant surroundings were thought to soften the rough edges of the urban poor and imbue them with a sense of civic pride. Furthermore, economic powerhouses, like Detroit, deserved to be grand.

As chair of Detroit's park commission, McMillan hired the legendary Frederick Law Olmsted of Central Park fame to turn the 980-acre Belle Isle in the middle of the Detroit River into a quiet, pastoral place for the people of ever-more crowded Detroit to enjoy. McMillan's peers thought Belle Isle was a boondoggle and later resisted Olmsted's designs, but McMillan persisted and used his own money, as he often would when he met resistance to his priorities.

This was true in politics too. McMillan was a Republican. At one time disgruntled, he reengaged with the party and organized a consortium of veterans, iron and ore miners, business leaders, and residents in the Upper Peninsula of Michigan, where many of his business interests lay. This "McMillan Alliance" and his $400,000 contribution consolidated his influence in legislative affairs around the state. Purportedly, he could kill any legislation he did not like, forcefully and quietly, or, conversely, get legislation passed. Marie Heyda, a Michigan historian, argues that McMillan and his rail-roads directly benefited from tax breaks approved by the state legis-lature, which he controlled.

But McMillan was not easily categorized, in part because of his friendly and calm demeanor. As a Lincoln Republican, he believed that individual and societal improvements were linked—thus the improvements on Belle Isle and the support for African-American college women—but he also believed in laissez-faire economics, a hallmark of the Democrats at that time. Having produced so many jobs in an unregulated marketplace, his belief in the latter was not surprising.

He assiduously cultivated friends from both parties, placing Democrats in many managerial positions within his companies and on boards and commissions he influenced. With the unanimous support of both parties in the state legislature, McMillan went to Washington, DC as the Republican Senator. It was 1889 and he was 51 years old.

MR. MCMILLAN GOES TO WASHINGTON

One of the richest men in Washington, and soon one of the most powerful, he built a house at the corner of Thomas Circle and Vermont Avenue; careful to avoid any appearance of financial con-flict, his house was the first and last financial investment he ever made in Washington, DC. His past professional experiences with railrods and steamships, however, made him a natural to serve on the powerful commerce, naval, and appropriations committees. But it was his service on the Senate Committee of the District of Columbia, a legislative bit player, that brought McMillan his greatest satisfaction and gave him a legacy.

In those days before locally elected officials, the chairman of that committee became the de facto mayor of Washington, DC. Familiar with urban issues—in addition to Detroit parks and his role in electoral politics—McMillan had served on the city's budget and appropriation committee.

In his first year as committee chair with nine Democrats and only one other Republican, McMillan and his colleagues passed 10 percent of all the laws Congress passed that year. Many helped ordinary people, from adding a plumbing inspector to ensuring one-fare streetcars to beginning to eliminate Washington's notorious back alleys.

McMillan's most significant contribution, however, coincided with the city's belated celebration of its 100th birthday. Everyone from senators to congressmen to veterans to newspaper editors to engineers and architects—in DC and nationwide—had ideas how best to mark that anniversary and transform a shabby and unimpressive capitol into something grand, befitting America's new role in the world.

The jockeying was frantic. The DC Board of Trade mounted an event, complete with an American flag in electric lights, to advance its idea for a memorial bridge; others wanted to enlarge the White House; others called for the redesign of the Mall. The American Institute of Architects (AIA) called for connections among parks and new guidelines for public buildings. The US Army Corps of Engineers had ideas and influence. Who would decide, who would pay, and how quickly could they do it? President McKinley turned to Senator McMillan, the "peacemaker of the senate," to figure it out. It was February 1900. McMillan accepted.

A MASTERFUL PROCESS

Some leaders conceive new ideas; others implement them. McMillan's genius was knowing a good idea when he heard it, and then making it happen. The chair of the American Institute of Architects suggested that the Chicago World's Fair of 1893 be the model for the centennial, and McMillan leapt.

The Chicago World's Fair was a temporary but elegant phenomenon of urban beautification, which had brought Chicago worldwide prestige and stature. It was the perfect idea for the centennial, but McMillan had to convince others that it was the perfect model. Process became key.

By mid-May, a joint resolution in Congress, advanced by McMillan, gave McMillan the authority to hire designers, and he quickly showed a sensitivity to both tradition and an orderly process. He said Pierre L'Enfant's 1791 original design for the city was sacrosanct.

L'Enfant, the French designer who won George Washington's trust, envisioned the city as a grid, cut by wide, diagonal boulevards, punctuated with public squares. The plan, without proper oversight and guidance, had long since been sullied. But McMillan knew that building on the old to make the new would reassure people of continuity, even if, as historian Jon Peterson writes, "few people other than architects knew or cared much about L'Enfant's idea."

Second and equally important, McMillan knew that L'Enfant's original plan indirectly addressed the problematic and contentious issue of the railroad tracks that ran down the middle of what he imagined might be a grand boulevard. He kept that to himself.

Third, McMillan knew he needed Daniel Burnham, the Chicago genius behind the World's Fair, who famously stated, "Make no little plans. They have no magic to stir men's blood." The other team members were the equally creative architect Charles F. McKim, the sculptor Augustus Saint-Gaudens, and the landscape architect Frederick Law Olmsted Jr. (whose father designed Central Park in New York and Belle Isle in Detroit).

McMillan hired them, but he positioned them as consultants who would present options but not have the final word. He also announced their combined fees would not exceed $10,000, and yet he assured them privately that he would personally pay the difference up to $20,000, if necessary. His fellow senators, relieved they were still in control, were supportive. (Ultimately the Senate paid the entire design fee of $54,000.)

Then McMillan appointed his trusted chief of staff, Charles Moore, to be secretary and project manager to the entire effort—keeping McMillan abreast, the designers' massive egos in check, and the work on track. This was vital.

Next was the buy-in. Relationships matter. McMillan hosted dinners at his house for the designers to meet President McKinley, key senators, cabinet members, and local power brokers.

Working from four different cities (Washington, Chicago, Boston, and New York) without the benefit of modern communications, the designers worked feverishly for ten months. They first assessed what had gone wrong with L'Enfant's original plan—the Washington Monument was off-kilter, and railroad station tracks, a hodgepodge of Victorian structures, and poorly placed trees desecrated the Mall. They agreed that the city parks were disconnected and inaccessible and, along with Moore, they traveled to Europe for six weeks to study architecture, parks, and boulevards. McMillan stayed behind justifying their "junket." People thought McMillan was a sucker, but he ignored the criticism.

He focused on the Pennsylvania Railroad and the Baltimore and Ohio Railroad, which together presented the greatest obstacle. The railroads had separate, unsightly stations on the Mall, which their railroad tracks divided and scarred. Changing the relationship and the operations of two competing railroads required money and co-operation, neither of which the companies wanted to contribute. Behind the scenes, McMillan began to negotiate new arrangements with the two railroads, asking them to abandon their terminals and tracks and share one station located near the Capitol in an area called "Swampoodle." He promised the railroad executives he'd work to convince Congress to help pay for the new station, bridges, viaducts, yards, and tunnels. After much discussion and cajoling, including a weekend at McMillan's summer home, the railroad executives, trusting McMillan's ability to deliver, agreed.

Typical of Burnham's expansive—and expensive—ideas, he wanted a grand exhibit to show off the final design. McMillan knew that an enthusiastic response to the vision was essential for future political and financial support, so he personally paid the lion's share for elaborate 3D models built from 10,000 wooden pieces, detailed maps, and 180 photographs and illustrations.

On January 15, 1902 (just four months after President McKinley died from an assassin's bullets), Senator McMillan escorted President Theodore Roosevelt through an extravagant exhibit at the Corcoran Art Gallery. The next day, the public poured in and loved it. Newspapers raved about it and, within four days, the *New York Times* predicted that Washington, DC "would become the most beautiful city in the world." The nationally influential *Century Magazine* wrote, "The more these plans and pictures are studied, the more thorough, the more magnificent, the nobler, do they seem."

President Theodore Roosevelt and his party view the models of the McMillan plan.

The concept, reflecting the Beaux Arts aesthetic of the Chicago World's Fair, melded landscape design with municipal improvements, such as street cleaning and tree planting, and civic design that favored artistic street lamps, bridges, and park entrances. But beyond the combined aesthetics, the plan introduced the concept of comprehensive planning. Formerly, other than city sewers, water pipes, and occasional parks, cities grew without plans or visions. Fragmentation ruled: factories placed anywhere spewed filth, rivers became garbage dumps, and unpaved streets kicked up dust or sunk in mud. Cities were ugly and unhealthy places.

The McMillan Plan, as it quickly became known, kept L'Enfant's grid and sunburst avenues, but combined them with an interconnected, city-wide park system and a spectacular two-and-a-half-mile, unified open space, the Mall. The plan envisioned new public buildings on this open space, stripped of its hodgepodge aesthetic and unsightly tracks; one elegant railroad station would stand close by but not on top of it. The designers imagined new parkways linking the city's parks, historic forts, and even Mount Vernon. The McMillan Plan made the city an aesthetic whole, and the senator, unknowingly, advanced the nationwide City Beautiful Movement, described by historian William Wilson as "an appealing mixture of ebullience and exactitude."

Daniel Burnham, a notoriously demanding architect, wanted McMillan to push for the formation of a permanent panel to ensure the plan's implementation. McMillan agreed that oversight was necessary, but he argued the timing was wrong; asking for too much too soon would weaken the whole politically. The plan, he said, had to be implemented incrementally, starting with the railroad station. Riding on the enthusiasm of the public, McMillan quickly turned to Congress to argue for the funds to help remove the train tracks and build the new terminal. Then he died.

"I fell at once to wondering, fearfully, how seriously his irreplaceable loss would set back the movement upon which we have all set our hearts," wrote Olmsted to Charles Moore.

But the team members did not lose heart. Led by Moore, they lobbied ferociously, and in February 1903, Congress passed legislation for a new railroad terminal and allocated $3 million to remove the tracks. Daniel Burnham designed the station, and Union Station opened in 1907.

Meanwhile, Charles Freer, another wealthy industrialist from Detroit, promised to donate his entire art collection and the funds to build a museum on the new Mall in recognition of his old friend James McMillan. President Roosevelt, excited about how that museum would anchor the McMillan Plan, convinced the Smithsonian Institute to accept the Freer gift and underwrite its maintenance in perpetuity—a first in Washington. (Delayed by World War 1, the Freer Gallery opened in 1922.)

In 1910, after much lobbying, the federal government established the Fine Arts Commission, which would guide future development, according to the McMillan Plan. And so it was.

"The consummate artistry and professionalism of the designers . . . and their enduring commitment to implementation, fortified by the practical shrewdness of their backers, and plain good luck . . . brought success," wrote Kohler and Scott, editors of *Designing the Nation's Capital: The 1901 Plan for Washington, D.C.*, published by the US Commission on Fine Arts in 2006.

MCMILLAN'S NAME BURIED

Hazen Pingree, sometimes called Detroit's finest mayor, had already damaged McMillan's legacy. The times—and particularly the growing gap between the rich and the poor, and the concomitant labor unrest—saw dramatic reevaluations of corporate leaders and their self-interest. McMillan's complicated web of business connections, political power, and tax benefits coupled with strikes at some of his factories changed his image.

Pingree, first as Detroit's mayor and then Michigan's governor, turned against his former Republican colleague, condemning corporate greed and attacking McMillan personally. By the time Pingree and McMillan had both died (Pingree in 1901 and

McMillan in 1902), McMillan's portrait no longer hung in the state capitol and he had become the symbol of all that was wrong with Michigan politics. James McMillan faded into history, overshadowed by his neighbor Henry Ford. Detroit never erected a monument for McMillan and virtually forgot his name.

By 1909, however, 35 cities throughout the nation had completed comprehensive plans for their municipalities, adhering to the principles of the McMillan Plan with centralized grand civic buildings and interconnected park systems. In 1910, the first ever National Conference on Urban Planning, inspired by the 1901 plan, took place in Washington, DC.

MUNI ONE

and the Violent, Inglorious
Road to Public Transit

The California Gold Rush of 1849 became a metaphor for all things fast and hopeful, and San Francisco itself personified it. Seemingly overnight, San Francisco became the ninth largest city in America, with the finest city hall, the tallest buildings, the biggest department store, the grandest theater, the loosest brothels, and the most active opium dens in the West. A major financial capital, it had scores of powerful banks and wealthy bankers, its port gave reach to Asia, and busy factories manufactured ferryboats and freighters. These extraordinary opportunities for wealth created great opportunities—and incentives—for workers to organize too.

Just as quickly as the magnates built their Pacific Heights mansions, San Francisco workers built their unions. Many were '49ers who stayed west when their dreams of gold collapsed; they were a tough and radical lot and their mettle shaped the city. Mark Twain described them as "an assemblage of 200,000 young men—not simpering, dainty-kid gloved weaklings, but stalwart, muscular, young braves, brimful of push and energy . . ."

By 1850, sailors and carpenters in San Francisco had struck for higher wages; within three years, most workers had a ten-hour workday. By the turn of the century (way ahead of their eastern counterparts), more than 30,000 workers had organized themselves into 98 different but affiliated unions, often working together under the banner of "Organize, Demand and Strike."

Growing cities meant more people needed transportation to more workplaces and more neighborhoods. Both New York and Chicago, for instance, grew by 30 percent in the first decade of the 20th century, but the demand for public transportation grew by 100 percent. San Francisco was no exception.

Cities big enough to have such challenges sold franchises to private companies to provide public transportation in horse-drawn carriages and steam-powered cable cars, and then, beginning around 1900, in electric streetcars.

Some people made fortunes from transit: Private enterprise built the cars, private enterprise powered them, private enterprise ran them, and private interests benefited from the real estate around them. Private investment in urban infrastructure was massive and pressure to keep profits high was great.

It did not take long for cities—many with corrupt contracting practices—to face complaints about overcrowded cars and inadequate service from underpaid workers and disgusted riders. Consequently, many people distrusted private business in public services. Public ownership of public services, including mass transit, became a major thrust of this era. New York, Cleveland, and Chicago experimented with ways to combine public interests with private interests. In San Francisco, voters went so far as to enact a law that said public utilities "shall be gradually acquired and ultimately owned by the City . . ."

That one phrase discouraged additional private investment in the growth of the transit system in San Francisco and provided an opening for one well-capitalized company, United Railroad (URR), to control the entire scene. The company spent hundreds of thousands of dollars buying up other private franchises, and by 1902, it owned all but three of the San Francisco transit companies in the city.

As URR was busy controlling the streetcar business, some streetcar workers started a union in 1902. By winning a higher wage for the workers (who went from 21 cents to 25 cents an hour), offering medical benefits to their members, and mounting recreational activities, union membership quickly grew in number.

But URR was rapacious. To decrease its costs, increase the company's profits, and solidify his own fortune, Patrick Calhoun, United Railroad's president, wanted to expand the lines and power them with overhead electrical lines. The public hated the idea of unsightly wires; they wanted costlier but invisible underground conduits, and they wanted URR to pay for them. The debate raged, lawsuits ensued, strikes were threatened, and then the great earthquake of April 1906 struck and everything changed.

Within one minute, the brick buildings of the central business district crumbled, collapsing onto the streets below, ripping up rail lines, destroying water mains, and cracking gas pipes, setting off apocalyptic fires that burned the city for three days. Raucous, energetic, and prosperous San Francisco was reduced to rubble—3,000 to 5,000 people died; 250,000 were left homeless; and 500 blocks and 28,000 buildings were destroyed. The city that President Theodore Roosevelt dubbed "the Garden of the Lord" became a mass of rubble, a nightmare of loss, and, for some, a golden opportunity to exploit the city and its people.

Within ten days of the earthquake, a few streetcars, all owned by United Railroads, were operating on cleared and rebuilt rails, and powered by those detested overhead electric wires. URR had gotten what it wanted.

THE STRIKES OF 1907

After the earthquake and ensuing cataclysmic fires, thousands camped in tents in parks and many rushed to ferries and left the city for good. Clearing the rubble and reconstruction began quickly, and work was plentiful. But wages stayed low, housing prices skyrocketed, and public transportation was abysmal—even URR called it "abominable." The new Straphangers League started to protest the overcrowded streetcars and elected "Mr. De Long Stand, Mr. George Armstretch and Mr. Willing Toositt" as its officers.

"No Seat. No Fare," they yelled.

But there was nothing funny about the strikes that began in early January 1907. First, the electrical workers went out, demanding $6 a day, not $5 ($138 in today's dollars). Then the metal tradesmen and laundry workers walked, wanting an eight-hour day; then the telephone operators, who were mostly women, threatened to strike, and their organizers were immediately fired.

"Tie Up the Town" was the call of anger. Doing just that, 2,000 streetcar workers voted to strike, saying overcrowded conditions and long workdays (without overtime pay) endangered the public; they demanded $3 for an eight-hour day. In late April 1907, the engineers, firemen, motormen, trackmen, linemen, and repairmen stopped the trolleys and paralyzed the city.

Thousands of people were forced to walk everywhere, and businesses, already reeling from the effects of the earthquake, suffered. Three days into the strike, URR ordered six streetcars out of one of its barricaded garages—straight into picket lines. Enraged workers, picketing outside, smashed the streetcar windows with bricks, paving stones, and bottles. From inside the car barn, URR employees opened fire, killing two men and wounding twenty more. The battle lines were drawn.

An Injured Strikebreaker in San Francisco Receives Help, 1907

The strike continued. The Straphangers League mocked both sides; some unionists rode cars driven by scabs; and one prominent woman published an open letter blaming "cold-hearted, grasping avaricious Eastern policy . . . [that] cast[s] the frost of suspicion on everything." The mayor tried to mediate, but rumors that URR was "importing" Japanese, Italians, and Greeks to take the car men's jobs made talk difficult.

Patrick Calhoun was tough, relentless, and uncompromising. Born in South Carolina in 1856, blue blood ran in his veins—he was a descendant of both George Washington and John Calhoun. His father, a rich plantation owner, lost his fortune during the Civil War, and Patrick, a widely read, obsessive teenager, became a lawyer at nineteen years old in Atlanta. He ended up in Cleveland, making a fortune in railroad consolidation before moving to San Francisco. He would die bankrupt at age 60.

"The Car men are no longer employees of mine," Calhoun declared in August 1907. "I shall run those roads if I have to bring 2,000 men to do it."

And he did just that. He hired James Farley, "the best hated man in America."

STRIKEBREAKING AS A BUSINESS MODEL

A 33-year-old businessman from New York with a walrus mustache, a penchant for horse racing, and a big income, James Farley was born in 1874 in upstate New York. He left home as a teenager and bounced around, working first for a circus and then shoveling coal for a private streetcar company in Brooklyn. There he experienced his first streetcar strike, and later in Philadelphia, while working for management during another streetcar strike, he was beaten by angry workers. He emerged from the hospital, healed but intent on starting a new strikebreaking business.

Strikes were an inevitable step in quickly industrializing an aggressively capitalistic America—and strikebreaking was an attractive business as profits soared and workers organized. Unlike other companies such as Pinkerton that were already in the strikebreaking businesses, Farley specialized in the booming private streetcar business. A supposedly genial man without great physical strength, but an iron will, legendary fearlessness, and a .38 always strapped to his belt, Farley opened his New York office in 1902. Over the next several years, he and his freelance scabs crushed some twenty to thirty strikes.

Farley said he liked unions; in fact, he claimed never to have worked for any railroad or streetcar company that paid its workers less than $2 a day, which was above average nationally. For Farley, strikebreaking was purely a business proposition, not an ideological mission.

"If I didn't do it someone else would," he said. Farley purportedly made a million dollars working for URR in San Francisco.

Farley telegraphed his 35 private detectives who monitored local labor scenes for him in major cities. Their job was to look for union rumblings, spot trouble, often before the companies did, and then coordinate men who made up Farley's "bunch," an elite group of freelance scabs. The scabs included college-educated men, doctors, ex–football players, and former union activists, disillusioned by some of the corrupt practices they witnessed among union leaders. Many worked full-time on the railroads—until they didn't. They were a footloose group.

"It is quite remarkable how far a man will travel . . . to get into a fight or for some excitement . . ." Farley once said. He paid his strikebreakers a bit more than whatever the local workers earned.

Loaded with medical supplies, enough food and beer to last four days, and 1,100 revolvers with 75,000 rounds of ammunition, three special trains left New York, Jersey City, and Philadelphia carrying 1,500 men—one of the largest gathering of scabs ever in America—heading to one of the toughest union towns in the nation.

In Chicago, the trains stopped to pick up additional strikebreakers. Hundreds of local workers, loyal to the San Francisco car men, pelted the railcars with stones and bricks, delaying the trains and, if reports are to be believed, scaring off a dozen or so strikebreakers. In Ogden, Utah, angry unionists met the trains again.

In San Francisco, the strikebreakers stayed in URR's car barns and they kept the trolleys running—most of the time—often accompanied by police guards. The strike lasted 131 days, with accidents occurring repeatedly—including one trolley that left the rails and flew into the air—and violence erupting frequently. By the time the union announced defeat in March 1908, 31 people had died in accidents or violence and more than 250 had been injured.

POLITICAL SCANDAL

Through all this, and in part because of it, political scandal erupted. The overhead electrical wires that appeared after the earthquake led to the truth. In June 1907, Mayor Eugene Schmitz was indicted on 27 counts of graft and bribery, including taking money from Patrick Calhoun to hang those power lines.

Schmitz, a musician with a winning smile and endless charm, was the puppet of the powerful political boss Abraham Ruef. A prodigy who finished Berkeley and law school before he was 21, Ruef started his professional life as a reformer, but enjoyed power and money more than social change. In 1901, he had established the United Labor Party, waving the banner of, and then exploiting, the working class. He and his political flunky, Eugene Schmitz, had bribed and blackmailed criminals as well as honest men. In spite of a damning public report, Mayor Schmitz was reelected for a second term, supported by those who believed he was on their side and those who benefited from his tricks.

But when a tough and independent prosecuting attorney, who had once shot a man to death in self-defense and would himself be shot by a disgruntled potential juror, went after Schmitz and Ruef, things toppled over. Ruef went to prison, Schmitz spent time in and out of courtrooms and jails, and then the political machine of San Francisco collapsed, leading to, among other things, the first publicly owned transportation system in the nation.

MUNI BEGINS

San Franciscans liked the idea of public ownership of public utilities—their charter, after all, allowed it—but taking over utilities from private companies required political will as well as money. In

December 1909, the voters elected a mayor who had the will and finally, after four earlier tries, the money when he convinced the voters to approve a bond issue.

United Railroad threw up numerous legal barriers to block the issuance of the bonds, and the banks were hesitant to purchase them. Eventually, small local investors bought the bonds, and the city finally assumed control of one private streetcar company when its franchise expired. In August 1911, hailed by boisterous revelers banging pots and pans, workers began digging up Geary Street—by hand—to prepare a new streetcar route.

A local, inexperienced company won the contract to manufacture new streetcars, but was only able to deliver 10 of the 43 cars the city had ordered. But that did not stop 50,000 people, who gathered along the route on December 28, 1912, as the first city-owned streetcar rolled out of the new city-owned and operated car barn.

"Let's get the cars going . . . and toot our horn afterward," suggested a cautious Mayor "Sunny Jim" Rolphe. But when he dropped his nickel into the fare box and the conductor rang the bell, the crowd erupted enthusiastically and the mayor found his confidence, proclaiming, "It is . . . the people's road, built by the people with the people's money . . . it is but the nucleus of a great system . . . which will one day encompass the entire City."

With a band playing, the first municipally owned and operated public streetcar began its journey. Big shots joined the mayor, uninvited men hung off the car, and souvenir hunters placed pennies on the tracks to be crushed. The motorman and conductor, both former employees of URR who had been fired for striking, guided Muni One down the tracks. Nine other trolleys followed in eight-minute intervals and some 20,000 people rode the trolleys that first day—some late into the night as firecrackers rattled the sky.

MUNI GROWS

By 1912, more people lived in San Francisco than had before the earthquake—about 420,000. Mayor Rolphe and his chief engineer knew one trolley line does not make a system, so they hired

Chicago's Bion J. Arnold, the preeminent transportation consultant, to devise a plan for Muni's expansion. Urgency was their priority.

No new profession in America was more fundamental to the growth of cities than civil and electrical engineers; they envisioned, designed, and built massive public works from water systems to dams to parks to electric railways. An inventor by nature, an electrical engineer by training, and an organizational genius by temperament, Arnold analyzed every physical, financial, and political aspect of the city's current and future transportation conditions—as he had for many other places—and in March 1913 he submitted his report.

Yes, San Francisco could implement a comprehensive municipal system, but it would take much work, he wrote, offering specific and comprehensive recommendations: Strengthen the charter language, renegotiate the franchises, dig new tunnels through the hills, standardize track widths, increase them by seventy miles, be honest about expenses and revenues, and increase the maintenance allowance. A tall order, for sure.

He assumed the public would read his report and warned them about placing unrealistic demands on the system; he even lectured them about proper trolley etiquette. Perhaps most significant, Arnold stressed the potential of the upcoming World's Fair.

President Taft had chosen San Francisco to host the Panama-Pacific Exposition to commemorate the opening of the Panama Canal. With financial help from the US Congress, San Francisco would turn 650 acres of wetlands along the bay into solid land. A colorful collection of massive pavilions showcasing states around the nation and countries around the world, miles of landscaped walkways, and a busy midway with fun and fancy would celebrate San Francisco's resilience and America's ingenuity.

URR, still with its franchises, refused to extend its streetcar service to accommodate the expected crowds, so Muni did. It built another new trolley line right to the front of the fairgrounds in time for the opening of the fair in February 1915. A huge success, the exposition attracted 18 million people, including many locals who went repeatedly and who reached the fantastical fairgrounds on the city-owned trolley line.

Nine months later, the temporary fairgrounds—including, ironically, an efficient and fast Ford Motor assembly line, a harbinger of things to come—were dismantled. The fair was gone, but San Francisco claimed a new residential neighborhood down along the bay for its growing population, complete with a convenient public trolley. San Francisco was back and the nation's first municipal transit system was moving forward. In 1944, URR relinquished its last franchise.

REFLECTIONS

on Public Service Leadership

The civic pioneers featured in this book lived and worked when the pace and breadth of innovation and industrialization changed every aspect of American life. Every person and every place at that time was impacted. Farmers moved and cities grew. Some middle-class white women and a few African Americans, both men and women, moved up and out, but never without a struggle. Immigrants from a wide array of nations arrived, dramatically adding to the nation's heterogeneity. The ostentatious lifestyles of Gilded Age oligarchs magnified the injustice of low wages and dangerous work for the many. Muckrakers gave life to it all.

These societal and economic swirls swept in new beliefs: that active government can—and should—deliver a better life for the greatest number; that what matters in public life is competence and merit, not politics or special interests; that unregulated business exploits workers and cheats consumers; that policy and practice should reflect knowledge rather than assumptions or prejudices; and that, more than anything, the common good matters. The civic entrepreneurs in this book responded to those challenges and embraced those values. They made America great.

These people came from around the country, but Chicago was often their touchstone. Chicago manifested the changes and challenges of the day; industrialization drove a shift from farming to factories, changing daily life, health, and culture. Into that tumultuous and often troubled mix came Hull House, the Chicago Woman's Club, and the University of Chicago.

The newly established university competed with the established institutions of the east, but unlike them, it stepped out of the ivory tower and encouraged applied research, using Chicago as its laboratory. It spearheaded social innovation and interdisciplinary study, and drew many of the most committed social and economic reformers, either as graduate students or teachers: Barnard, Flagg Young, Davis, Kellor, and Vollmer among them. Furthermore, Barnard, Lindsey, Kellor, Lathrop, and Davis had direct connections with Chicago's Hull House, which often collaborated with the Chicago Woman's Club where Lucy Flower was active. The synergy among these institutions was electric in tone and national in impact.

Beyond Chicago, these leaders shared other traits. What were they?

1. *Their commitment to the common good rather than to ideology was undeniable.* Each, of course, had his or her own personality, from the quiet to the quirky, the shy to the flamboyant. Some were more personally ambitious than others—Waring, Dewey, and Lindsey, in particular—but they all possessed a passion bigger than themselves that drove their individual commitments.

2. *Perseverance and, in most cases, courage ran through their veins.* McMillan was dogged in the face of conflicting agendas. Mulholland spent years, often in the field himself, building an aqueduct 230 miles long through rugged terrain. Waring, a veteran of hand-to-hand combat in the Civil War, took a job others thought beneath him to do what most considered undoable. Swenie never sent his men into fires that he himself wouldn't fight. Davis refused to build fences around Bedford Hills. Kellor traveled alone through the racist South, asking intimate questions of both black and white women.

3. *They were all problem-solvers.* Although they approached challenges from different angles, they all identified specific problems within their chosen fields. They identified these problems—some unacknowledged or unknown—based on fact and reality rather

than on assumptions and prejudices. They then set about addressing the problems energetically and practically. They did so, respecting data and honoring experience.

4. *They were insatiably curious.* Their educational backgrounds varied. Three of the women and the African American man were college educated; two of the women had PhDs. Formal education was not a factor in the accomplishments of the white men, however. Swenie, Mulholland, Lindsey, Waring, Vollmer, and McMillan had little education beyond high school, if that. By dint of their positions, they interacted with power brokers, but most were not themselves "the educated elite." What they all shared—men and women, with or without a formal education—was an eagerness to learn.

Mulholland taught himself hydro-engineering and geology in a shack at night. Waring learned the science of drainage by looking and listening. Vollmer "stole" good ideas wherever he found them. Flagg Young taught herself to read and, as an adult, set aside three nights a week to study. Mayo spent his holidays visiting other hospitals, and Kellor and Davis, both with PhDs, benefited from their scholarly aptitude. But, even without an academic's precision, they all exhibited voracious curiosity.

5. *They respected competence.* Swenie, Waring, and Flagg Young refused to hire or promote for political reasons; Kellor, Vollmer, Dewey, Blue, and Young were deeply committed to ongoing professional development.

6. *New thinking and new things did not scare them.* Technological innovation—or what the economist Robert J. Gordon calls the "great inventions"—came swiftly, and these people embraced them. Swenie saw value in fireboats and steam engines and trained his reluctant firefighters accordingly. Mulholland used, for a while at least, the newly developed Caterpillars to dig the desert sand. McMillan foresaw the importance of local transportation. Vollmer adapted everything from alarm systems to radio cars.

7. *They were entrepreneurial.* When Barnard struck a deal with her local Oklahoma City newspaper (support my time in Chicago and I will send articles about Chicago poverty), she got money, the

paper got scoops, and together they informed readers about the potential ills of urbanization—something Oklahoma had not yet experienced. Dewey, keen to encourage utilitarian library design, established a purchasing cooperative to provide libraries with standard furniture and equipment at affordable rates. Mayo, while still a teenager, practiced surgery on the eyes of dead animals. Waring sold New York City grease to soap factories and horse manure to cotton plantations to increase the department's revenues and recycle the waste. Blue established satellite libraries. Lindsey became a volunteer probation officer.

8. *They all understood the importance of good communications.* Some used clever public relations to change perceptions. Waring dressed his sanitation workers in white and recruited poor kids to serve as ambassadors of cleanliness. Others were less flashy, but equally strategic. Mulholland needed a steady stream of hardy laborers, so his office released articles about the aqueduct for different audiences in different outlets all around the nation all the time. Barnard gave stem-winding speeches to rally public opinion. Kellor invited Lewis Hine, the famous photographer, on her visits to work camps. Vollmer gave newspaper reporters desks and easy access to police files. Many wrote books and articles, including Vollmer, Kellor, and Davis; and Lindsey became a muckraker. They all understood that without public support government cannot work.

9. *They questioned authority when necessary and talked back to power when needed.* Some spoke loudly—Waring, Barnard, and Lindsey—or, in the case of Swenie, forcefully, if not loudly. Others moved ahead purposefully, arguing against accepted but bad practices: Young, Davis, and Kellor. One was notably quiet—McMillan—but proceeded even when other powerful people mocked him. One exception was Dewey. When he defied Columbia's policy and enrolled women, one wonders if it was for principle or sexual amusement.

10. Apart from Colonel Waring and Senator McMillan, *they all eschewed the mad march to materialism that aggressive capitalism produces.* With their inventiveness and diligence, many might have

enjoyed the boom-boom days of the business world and played with the perks of the Gilded Age. But they saw public service as their reward, not a path to greater riches.

Many ended their careers with dignity: Vollmer, Swenie, Waring, Kellor, McMillan, and Mayo. But several paid a steep price for their work. Both Flagg Young and Davis were forced to resign (or be fired) because of their open pursuit of facts, and Mulholland resigned in disfavor after the devastating collapse of the St. Francis Dam.

Dewey, Lindsey, and Barnard are more complicated. Dewey seemed uncaring about the accusations of sexual harassment, which ended his career as a librarian. Lindsey won national praise for his campaign for juvenile courts, but he never tempered his undifferentiated and sometimes self-defeating attacks on all Denver elites and so found himself without many defenders when he burned court papers or made questionable decisions about his personal life. Barnard's relentless fight was righteous and justified, but her personal anger subsumed her good sense and likely caused debilitating stress.

I spent lots of time with these people and I have my favorites: Katherine Bement Davis, Charlie Mayo and August Vollmer. All three were self-assured, but not egotistical; they were innovative and farsighted, but not messianic. Mayo was unpretentious with a nice sense of humor; Vollmer, always modest, shared the spotlight with his cops; and Davis, a risk-taker, was intentional and fearless.

I admired Frances Kellor, who not only pursued social justice professionally, but also presented herself without apparent shame or braggadocio. I stand in awe of William Mulholland's ingenuity and am impressed by Denis Swenie's physical courage. I like Thomas Blue's maturity. Ben Lindsey's ego bugged me and Kate Barnard's loneliness unsettled me. I admired James McMillan's bipartisanship, but I didn't warm up to flamboyant Waring. Ella Flagg Young, as her father once said, was a tad humorless, and Melvil Dewey was obnoxious, if not downright offensive.

But all of them—every single one—impressed me with their commitment to the common good and their desire to make government work. They were dogged pioneers on the civic frontier.

Today we are in the throes of another technological revolution. Automation, artificial intelligence, and robotics are disrupting methods of production and avenues to employment. Heavily trafficked roads and bridges collapse, even as a few purchase tickets on private rockets to outer space. Affordable housing, good medical care, and strong education are elusive, even for the middle class, as the earth warms, ice melts, and irreversible climate change threatens our existence. These times beg again for visionary leaders on all levels of government. May a new generation of civic pioneers emerge, embracing the shared traits of their descendants.

ACKNOWLEDGMENTS

Writing this book has been a total treat, and thanks go to many. They start with Bill Zinsser, my wonderful writing teacher, who gave me this idea.

"You know something about city government. Teach me something I do not know," the endlessly curious Zinsser said. "Find dramatic people who built our cities. Surprise me." He heard two chapters before he died; I hope he would be pleased by the rest.

My old charter revision buddy Eileen Sullivan, a political scientist by training and a gifted teacher by vocation, helped me throughout. She suggested that I stay away from the academic boxing ring and not look for the best or the first, and underscored Bill's advice to find the dramatic and the creative. She pointed me toward the turn of the 20th century when activist government began, and that's where I remained. Other friends in the academic world were supportive and helpful at various points along the way; I thank, in particular, Morris Rossabi, Jeremy Travis, Leslie Newman, Chad Berry, and Gerry Benjamin.

The inimitable Jay Barksdale at the New York Public Library gave me a key to the Wertheim Study with my own private shelf for books on extended loan, a table, and exquisite quiet—to say nothing of easy access to other endlessly helpful librarians including his able successor, Melanie Locay. I am deeply appreciative of my three years there.

As Bill would have wanted, I visited many of the places where these pioneers worked. The rich resources in New York, Los Angeles, San Francisco, Chicago, and Washington, DC did not surprise me, and I am sorry I never got to Denver or Louisville. But

Guthrie, Oklahoma; Rochester, Minnesota; and the Owens Valley in California brought Barnard, Mayo, and Mulholland alive for me in ways books or museums cannot do. Seeing Andrew Carnegie's unpretentious grave in Sleepy Hollow, New York, was as meaningful as visiting his mansion on Fifth Avenue.

Did God ever invent a more curious and accommodating group of people than archivists at history museums? I doubt it. I want to pay special tribute to Laura Martin at the Oklahoma History Research Center, Michael Williams at the Oklahoma Territorial Museum in Guthrie, and John Walker at the First Baptist Church of Newalla, Oklahoma. Nancy Adgent at the Rockefeller Archive Center in Sleepy Hollow was the consummate professional. Jon Kusmire and Roberta Harlan at the Eastern California Museum in Independence, California, made my trip to the Owens Valley productive and pleasant. Although we never met, Elson Trinidad's web-based guide of the Los Angeles Aqueduct was invaluable for this California-shy driver. Renee Ziemer at the W. Bruce Fye Center for the History of Medicine in Rochester, Minnesota, was extremely knowledgeable, and Emily Christopherson at the Mayo Historical Suite and Krista Lewis at the History Center of Olmsted County were both most accommodating. I hope I have not forgotten anyone.

Someone once said, "Never take a book to lunch." I try to heed that advice, but when I forgot, many friends and family members were patient with my obsessions. Thanks to Jack Goldstein, Mary Rossabi, Susan Herman, Karen Blessen, Linda Lange, Joel Copperman, Cathy McDowell, Kate Dunning, Alex Wardle, Ned York, Sylvia Yee, Brian McCaffrey, Jean Marzollo (RIP), Michele Hilmes, Vicky Streitfeld, Michelle Woods, Nat Leventhal, Gene Russianoff, Pauline Toole, Joanie Omeste, Suany Chough, Franci Wiener, Tom O'Connor, Lisa Berry, Jeff McHugh, Cliff Chanin, Justine McGovern, Alison Dykstra, Andrew Schulman, Tina Mead, David Mead and Robert Love. Some of the guys I tutor at a local prison gave me helpful feedback, and my mother was endlessly interested in both the people and my process—even in her 98th year.

I hope they all find these pioneers worth the time they spent with them and me.

Thanks to April Eberhardt, Laura Zats and Graham Warnken, and all their colleagues at Wise Ink, Stephanie Marohn, Kelly Figueroa-Ray, Rachel Adams, and Greg Hughes for caring about making the book as good as it can be and finding an audience for it.

And, finally, again, to Bill Zinsser and his irreplaceable gift of friendship and guidance. I'd swear he's perched on my shoulder, wearing his baseball cap, encouraging me to stay focused, uncluttered, and on the road! Thanks, Bill. I miss you.

BIBLIOGRAPHY

GENERAL

Allen, Frederick Lewis. *The Big Change: American Transforms Itself, 1900–1950.* New York: Harper, 1952.

Dinnerstein, Leonard, and David Reimers. *Ethnic Americans: A History of Immigration.* New York: Columbia University Press, 2009.

Gordon, Robert. *The Rise and Fall of American Growth.* Princeton: Princeton University Press, 2016.

Griffith, Ernest S. *A History of American City Government: The Progressive Years and Their Aftermath, 1900-1920.* Praeger, 1974.

Gunther, John. *Inside U.S.A.* New York: Harper, 1946.

Hofstadter, Richard. *The Age of Reform.* New York: Vintage Books, 1955.

Kennedy, John F. *Profiles in Courage.* New York: Harper, 1956.

Lears, Jackson. *Rebirth of a Nation: The Making of Modern America, 1877–1920.* New York: HarperCollins, 2009.

Leonard, Thomas. *Illiberal Reformer.* Princeton: Princeton University Press, 2016.

McGerr, Michael. *A Fierce Discontent: The Rise and Fall of the Progressive Movement in America.* New York: Oxford University Press, 2005.

O'Donnell, Edward. *Henry George, Labor and the Gilded Age.* www.c-span.org

Pomper, Gerald M. *On Ordinary Heroes and American Democracy.* Boulder: Paradigm, 2007.

Schlereth, Thomas. *Victorian America: Transformation of Everyday Life, 1876–1915.* New York: Harper Perennial, 1991.

Spain, Daphne. *How Women Saved the City.* Minneapolis: University of Minnesota Press, 2001.

Steffens, Lincoln. *The Shame of the Cities.* New York: McClure, Phillips, 1904.

Teaford, Jon C. *The Twentieth-Century American City.* Baltimore: Johns Hopkins University Press, 1993.

Teaford, Jon C. *The Unheralded Triumph of City Government, 1870–1900.* Baltimore: Johns Hopkins University Press, 1984.

Ware, Susan. *American Women's History.* New York: Oxford University Press, 2015.

White, Richard. *Railroaded: The Transcontinentals and the Making of Modern America.* New York: W.W. Norton, 2011.

CHAPTER 1: KATE BARNARD

Barnard, Kate. "Human Ideals in State Government." *Survey* Vol. 23 (October 1909–March 1910).

Bennett, Helen Christian. *American Women in Civic Work.* Dodd, Mead, 1919.

Burke, Bob, and Glenda Carlile. *Kate Barnard: Oklahoma's Good Angel.* Edmond: University of Central Oklahoma, 2001.

Crawford, Suzanne Jones, and Lynn Musslewhite. "Kate Barnard, Progressivism and the West," in *An Oklahoma I Had Never Seen Before: Alternative Views of Oklahoma History,* edited by Davis D. Joyce. Norman: University of Oklahoma Press, 1994.

Debo, Angie. *And Still the Waters Run.* Princeton: Princeton University Press, 1940.

Department of Charities and Corrections. *Second Report 1909–1910.* Kate Barnard Papers. Oklahoma City: Oklahoma Historical Society.

Goble, Danny. *Progressive Oklahoma: The Making of a New Kind of State*. Norman: University of Oklahoma Press, 1980.

Leavitt, Julian. *The Man in the Cage. American* Magazine Vol. 73 (1912).

"Little Miss Kate Makes Women Weep." *New York Tribune,* December 1, 1912.

Logan, Jim. "Saint Kate." *Oklahoma Today*, November/December 2012.

Marsh, Ralph. "Crusader Kate." *Oklahoma Today*, December 1989.

Musslewhite, Lynn, and Suzanne J. Crawford. *One Woman's Political Journey: Kate Barnard and Social Reform, 1875–1930*. Norman: University of Oklahoma Press, 2003.

Reese, Linda William. *Women of Oklahoma, 1890–1920*. Norman: University of Oklahoma Press, 1997.

"Woman Sees Plot to Rob Indians." *New York Times,* November 14, 1914.

"Working to Stop Robbery of Indians." *New York Times*, November 15, 1914.

CHAPTER 2: DENIS SWENIE

Aftermath. Curious City Series. Chicago: www.WBEZ.org.

Andreas, Alfred. *History of Chicago*. Chicago: A. T. Andreas, 1884.

Bales, Richard. *The Great Chicago Fire and the Myth of Mrs. O'Leary's Cow*. Jefferson, NC: McFarland, 2002.

Chicago Historical Society. "Swenie, The Fire-fighter." www.chicagohistory.org

Chicago Historical Society. "The Great Chicago Fire." www.chicagohistory.org

Colbert, David. *Eyewitness to America*. New York: Pantheon, 1997.

Cosgrove, Bill. *Chicago's Forgotten Tragedy*. Bloomington, IN: Author House, 2010.

Cromie, Robert. *The Great Chicago Fire*. New York: McGraw-Hill, 1958.

Fanning, Charles. *Finley Peter Dunne and Mr. Dooley: The Chicago Years*. Lexington: University Press of Kentucky, 2014.

Hill, Charles. *Fighting a Fire*. New York: Century, 1900.

History of Insurance. www.economichistory.net

History of the Chicago Fire Insurance Patrol. www. ChicagoFirePatrol.com

Jennings, Herbert T. *Bucket Brigade to Flying Squadrons: Fire Fighting Past and Present*. George Ellis, 1909.

Johnson, Ray. "The July 10, 1893 World's Columbia Expo Cold Storage Fire." www.ChicagoNow.com

Leslie, Thomas. *Chicago Skyscrapers, 1871–1934*. Champaign: University of Illinois Press, 2013.

Lewis, Arnold. "Discovering Chicago's Architecture," in *An Early Encounter with Tomorrow: Europeans, Chicago's Loop, and the World's Columbian Exposition*. Champaign: University of Illinois Press, 1997.

Perry, Robert. *Facts and Observations on the Sanitary State of Glasgow, 1844*. Glasgow University Library Special Collections.

Thornton, Willis. *The Nine Lives of Citizen Train*. Greenberg Publishers, 1948.

Train, George Francis. *My Life in Many States and Foreign Lands*. New York: Appleton, 1902.

CHAPTER 3: COLONEL GEORGE WARING

Burnstein, Daniel Eli. *Next to Godliness: Confronting Dirt and Despair in Progressive Era New York*. Champaign: University of Illinois, 2006.

Cassedy, James. "The Flamboyant Colonel Waring." *Bulletin of the History of Medicine* Vol. 36, No. 2 (March-April, 1962).

Dowdy, Wayne. *A Brief History of Memphis*. Charleston, SC: History Press, 2011.

Experiment Station Record, Vol. 10. Washington DC: US Printing Office, 1899.

Hughes, C. J. "A Lab, A Home, A Memory." *New York Times,* August 4, 2012.

James, A. R. *Standard History of Memphis, Tennessee.* H. W. Crew, 1912.

Jones, Maria M. *Protecting Public Health in New York City: 200 Years of Leadership, 1805–2005.* New York City Department of Health and Mental Hygiene, 2005.

"The Military Element in Colonel Waring's Career." *Century Magazine* Vol. 59 (February 1900).

Nagle, Robin. *Picking Up: On the Streets and Behind the Trucks with the Sanitation Workers of New York City.* New York: Farrar, Straus and Giroux, 2013.

Personal Hygiene in America. Winterthur, DE: Winterthur Museum, Garden and Library, 2009.

Rice, Kevin. *Dignity and Respect: The History of Local 831.* New York: Uniformed Sanitationmen's Association, 2009.

Rosenzweig, Roy, and Elizabeth Blackmar. *The Park and the People: A History of Central Park.* Ithaca, NY: Cornell University, 1992.

Schladweiler, Jon C. "Water Resources Programs Benefit from Sewer History." *APWA Reporter,* February 2007.

Shaw, Dr. Albert. *Life of Colonel George E. Waring, Jr.* New York Patriotic League, 1899.

Snay, Mitchell. *Horace Greeley and the Politics of Reform in Nineteenth Century America.* Lanham, MD: Rowman and Littlefield, 2011.

Waring, G. E., Jr. *Draining for Profit, and Draining for Health.* New York: Orange Judd, 1867.

Waring, G. E., Jr. *Street-Cleaning and the Disposal of a City's Wastes.* New York: Doubleday and McClure, 1897.

Waring, G. E., Jr. *Whip and Spur.* New York: Doubleday and McClure, 1897.

Waring Memorial Service. City and State Vol. 5 (December 1, 1898).

Zeliadt, Nicholette. "Talking Trash During the Dog Days: A Brief History of Sanitation in New York." *Scientific American,* July 2010.

CHAPTER 4: FRANCES KELLOR

Barrett, James. "Americanization from the Bottom Up: Immigrants and the Remaking of the Working Class in the United States, 1880–1930." *Journal of American History* Vol. 79, No. 3 (1998).

Cannato, Vincent. *American Passage: The History of Ellis Island.* New York: HarperCollins, 2009.

Commission of Immigration of the State of New York. *Final Report, 1908–1909.*

Davis, Philip, editor. *Immigration and Americanization.* Boston: Ginn and Co. 1920.

Hartman, Edward George. *The Movement to Americanize the Immigrant.* New York: Columbia University Press, 1948.

Higham, John. *Strangers in the Land.* New York: Atheneum, 1967.

Kellor, Frances. *The Immigrant Woman. Atlantic Monthly* Vol. 100, No. 3 (September 1907).

Kellor, Frances. *Immigration and the Future.* New York: George Dovan, 1920.

Kellor, Frances. "Psychological and Environmental Study of Women Criminals." *American Journal of Sociology,* January–March 1900.

Kellor, Frances. *Straight America, A Call to National Service.* New York: MacMillan, 1916.

Maxwell, William J. "Frances Kellor in the Progressive Era: A Case Study of the Professionalization of Reform." PhD Dissertation, Columbia University.

Miller, John J. *Profiles in Citizenship.* Policy Review, Hoover Institution, 1997.

Murdach, Allison. "Frances Kellor and the Americanization Movement." *Social Work* Vol. 53, No. 1 (January 2008).

New York State Bureau of Immigration and Industry. *Annual Report, 1910–1911.*

Press, John Kenneth. *Founding Mother: Frances Kellor and the Creation of Modern America.* New York: Social Books, 2012.

"Preying Upon Helpless Immigrants After They Land." *New York Times,* April 14, 1912.

Riis, Jacob. *How The Other Half Lives.* New York: Dover, 1971.

Wald, Lillian. *The House on Henry Street.* New York: Henry Holt, 1915.

Wald, Lillian, and Frances Kellor. *Construction Camps of the People Survey* 23 (January 1910).

Ziegler, Christina A. *Americanization in the States: Immigrant Social Welfare Policy and National Identity in the United States, 1908–1929.* University Press of Florida, 2009.

CHAPTER 5: AUGUST VOLLMER

Ashbury, Herbert. *The Barbary Coast: An Informal History of the San Francisco Underground.* Knopf, 1933.

August Vollmer: Pioneer in Police Professionalism. Regional Oral History Office, Bancroft Library, University of California, 1971–1972.

"August Vollmer Suicide." *New York Times,* November 5, 1955.

Gene E. and Elaine H. Carte. *Police Reform in the United States: The Era of August Vollmer.* Berkeley: University of California Press, 1975

Dempsey, John, and Linda Forst. "An Introduction to Policing." www.cengage.com

Ethington, Philip J. "Vigilantes and the Police: The Creation of a Professional Police Bureaucracy in San Francisco, 1847–1900." *Journal of Social History* Vol. 21 (Winter 1987).

Fosdick, Raymond B. "Modus Operandi System in the Detection of Criminals." *Journal of Criminal Law and Criminology* Vol. 6, No. 4 (1916).

Gourley, G. Douglas. *Public Relations and the Police.* Charles Thomas, 1953.

Henderson, George C. *Keys to Crookdom.* Appleton, 1924.

Oliver, Willard. *August Vollmer: The Father of American Policing.* Durham, NC: Carolina Academic Press, 2007.

Parker, Alfred E. *The Berkeley Police Story.* Springfield, IL: Charles Thomas, 1972.

Parker, Alfred E. *Crime Fighter: August Vollmer.* New York: MacMillan, 1961.

Potter, Gary. *The History of Policing in the United States.* Police Studies Online, www.eku.edu

Reppetto, Thomas. *American Police: The Blue Parade, 1845–1945.* New York: Enigma Books, 2010.

Schwartz, Richard. *Berkeley 1900: Daily Life at the Turn of the Century.* RSB Books, 2009.

"To Pit Educators vs. Gunmen." *New York Times,* May 19, 1929.

Vollmer, August. *The Criminal.* Foundation Press, 1949.

Vollmer, August, and Alfred Parker. *Crime, Crooks and Cops.* New York: Funk and Wagnalls, 1937.

Wilson, O. W. "August Vollmer." *Journal of Criminal Law, Criminology, and Police Science* Vol. 91 (1953–1954).

CHAPTER 6: LINDSEY, LATHROP, AND FLOWER

Addams, Jane. *My Friend, Julia Lathrop.* New York: MacMillan, 1935.

Barfoot, Charles H. *Aimee Semple McPherson and the Making of Modern Pentecostalism, 1890–1926.* London: Routledge, 2015.

Benjamin Barr Lindsey Papers, Manuscript Collection, Library of Congress.

"Ben Lindsey: A Crusader for Last 30 Years." *New York Herald Tribune,* December 8, 1930.

Borough, Reuben. "The Little Judge." *Colorado Quarterly* Vol. 16 (Spring 1968).

Campbell, D'Ann. "Judge Ben Lindsey and the Juvenile Court Movement 1901–1904." *Arizona and the West* Vol. 18, No. 1 (Spring 1976).

"The Children's Court." *New York Herald Tribune,* September 17, 1924.

Clapp, Elizabeth J. *Mothers of All Children: Women Reformers and the Rise of Juvenile Courts in Progressive Era America.* University Park, PA: Penn State University Press, 1998.

Denver Juvenile and Family Court. *The Court.* 1904.

Fox, Sanford J. "The Early History of the Court." *Future of Children* Vol. 6, No. 3 (Winter 1996).

Greusel, John H. "The Child Is the State." *New York Tribune,* September 6, 1908.

Iverson, Kristen. *Molly Brown: Unraveling the Myth.* Boulder, CO: Johnson Books, 1999.

"Julia Lathrop". www.vcencyclopedia.vassar.edu

Larsen, Charles. *The Good Fight.* Quadrangle Books, 1972.

Lindsey, Ben, and Rube Burrough. *The Dangerous Life.* Horace Liveright, 1931

Lindsey, Ben B, and Harvey J. O'Higgins. *The Beast.* New York: Doubleday Page and Co., 1910

Lindsey, Judge Ben B., and Evans Wainwright. *The Companionate Marriage.* Garden City Publishing Co., 1929.

Lindsey Disbarred in Colorado. *New York Herald Tribune,* December 10, 1929.

Nasaw, David. *Children of the City: At Work and Play.* New York: Doubleday, 1985.

National Park Service. *The New Empire of the Rockies: A History of Northeast Colorado. www.nps.gov/parkhistory., 2008*

Parker, Graham. "The Juvenile Court Movement: The Illinois Experience." *University of Toronto Law Journal* Vol. 26, No. 3 (Summer 1976).

Pinckney, Merritt W. *The Child in the City.* Department of Social Investigation, Chicago, 1912.

Shepherd, Robert E., Jr. "The Juvenile Court at 100 Years: A Look Back." *Juvenile Justice Journal* Vol. 6, No. 2 (December 1999).

Steffens, Lincoln. *Upbuilders.* New York: Doubleday, 1909.

Tanenhaus, David S. "Justice for the Child: The Beginning of the Juvenile Court in Chicago." *Chicago History Magazine,* Winter 1998–1999.

Tichi, Cecilia. *Justice, Not Pity: Julia Lathrop.* Library of Congress Lecture, June 28, 2007.

CHAPTER 7: KATHERINE BEMENT DAVIS

Beam, Alex. "The Naughty Professor." *Stanford Magazine,* September/October 1997.

Bell, Ernest. *Fighting the Traffic in Young Girls or War on the White Slave Trade.* Bell, 1910.

Bressan, David. "Messina Earthquake." *Scientific American,* December 28, 2012.

The Rockefeller Foundation: A Digital History. "Bureau of Social Hygiene," www.rockfound.rockarch.org (n.d.)

Davis, Katherine Bement. *Factors in the Sex Life of 2200 Women.* Harper, 1929.

Davis, Katherine Bement. "Relief Work for the Messina Refugees in Syracuse." *Survey* Vol. 22 (1909).

Davis, Katherine Bement. *Workingman's Model Home as exhibited by New York at the World's Columbia Exposition, 1893.*

"Dr. Katherine Bement Davis Honored at Dinner." *New York Times,* February 3, 1928.

Fahs, Breanne, Mary Dudy, and Sarah Stage. *The Moral Panics of Sexuality.* New York: Palgrave MacMillan, 2013.

Freedman, Estelle B. *Their Sisters' Keepers: Women's Prison Reform in America, 1930–1930*. University of Michigan Press, 1984.

Goldman, Emma. *Anarchism and Other Essays*, "The Traffic in Women," www.gutenberg.org, 1910.

"Island Voices Are Raised in Song." *New York Times,* July 13, 1914.

Katherine Bement Davis Papers, Rockefeller Archives, Sleepy Hollow, NY.

Kneeland, George J. *Commercialized Prostitution in New York City.* Bureau of Social Hygiene, Century, 1913.

McCarthy, Thomas. *A Mini-History of the Department's First Woman Head: Katherine Bement Davis.* New York City Department of Corrections, 1997.

McCarthy, Thomas. *New York City Corrections.* www. CorrectionHistory.org, 1997.

Mills, Herbert. *Course Outline: Study of the Dependent, Defective and Delinquent.* Vassar College, 1918.

"Miss Davis Puts No Faith in Luck: Eternal Vigilance Is the Secret of Success." *New York Times,* February 7, 1914.

Morris, Norval. *The Oxford History of the Prison.* Oxford University Press, 1998.

"Prominent People Talk about Greatest Temptations to Young." *New York Times,* November 20, 1916.

Roe, Clifford G. *The Great War on White Slavery or Fighting for the Protection of Our Girls.* W. L. Walter, 1911.

Sealander, Judith. *Private Wealth and Public Life: Foundation Philanthropy and the Reshaping of American Social Policy.* Johns Hopkins University Press, 1997.

Sladen, Douglas. *In Sicily, 1896–98–1900.* New York: Dutton, 1901.

"Survey Shows Why College Girls Stay Single." *New York Times,* February 18, 1928.

Tarbell, Ida. "Good Will to Woman." *American Magazine,* Vol. 75, 1912-23.

Tarbell, Ida. "Making a Man of Herself." *American Magazine,* Vol. 73, No. 1, 1911-12.

Turner, George Kibbe. "The City of Chicago: A Study of the Great Immoralities." *McClure's Magazine,* April 1907.

Turner, George Kibbe. "Daughters of the Poor." *McClure's Magazine,* November 1909.

"Women to Visit Miss Davis: Suffragists Will Congratulate New Commissioner of Corrections." *New York Times,* January 4–5, 1914.

"Women Turn to Democrats." *New York Times,* October 21, 1926.

CHAPTER 8: ELLA FLAGG YOUNG

"Crusade vs. Germs." *Chicago Tribune,* May 22, 1911.

Donatelli, Rosemary. "The Contributions of Ella Flagg Young to the Educational Enterprise." PhD dissertation, University of Chicago, 1971.

Flexner, Abraham. "A Modern School." *American Review of Reviews* Vol. 53 (1916).

Helge, Jan, and Paula Malak, editors. *The Greater Roseland Area of Chicago Schools.* South Suburban Genealogical and Historical Society, 1994.

Holcomb, Sabrina. "The History of the National Education Association." NEA.org (n.d.).

Knoll, Michael. "Dewey as Administrator: The Inglorious End of the Laboratory School in Chicago." *Journal of Curriculum Studies* Vol. 47.

McManis, John T. *Ella Flagg-Young and a Half-Century of the Chicago Public Schools.* A.C. McClurg, 1916.

"Mrs. Young Asks School Reform." *Chicago Daily Tribune,* July 12, 1911.

Reid, Robert. "The Professionalization of Teachers: The Chicago Experience, 1895–1920." PhD Dissertation, Northwestern University, 1968.

Rice, Joseph M. "The Public-School System of the United States." New York: Century. 1893.

Smith, Joan Karen. "Ella Flagg Young." PhD Dissertation, Ames, IA: Iowa State University, 1976.

Taylor, Graham. "Ella Flagg-Young: First Woman Superintendent of Chicago Schools and President of the National Education Association." *Survey* Vol. 24, no. 17 (July 23, 1910).

Volo, Dorothy D. *Children in Industrial America.* Daily Life through History. www.ABC-CLIO.com., 2015.

Winship, A. E. "Twenty-Five Years of Chicago." *Journal of Education* Vol. 71, No. 24 (June 16, 1910).

CHAPTER 9: DEWEY, CARNEGIE, AND BLUE

Bostwick, Arthur E. *American Public Library.* Appleton, 1910.

Butler, P. "Dewey-Casanova Syndrome." *New York Times Magazine,* October 17, 1976.

Carnegie, Andrew. *A Gospel to Wealth and Other Essays,* 1889.

Garrison, Dee. *Apostles of Culture: The Public Librarian and American Society, 1876–1920.* Madison, WI: University 0f Wisconsin Press, 2003

Elliott, Anna. "Melvil Dewey: A Singular and Contentious Life." *Wilson Library Bulletin,* May 1981.

Gleason, Eliza Atkins. *The Southern Negro and the Public Library.* University of Chicago Press, 1941.

Jones, Reinette F. *Library Service to African Americans in Kentucky.* Jefferson, NC: McFarland, 2002.

Kaestle, Carl F., and Janice A. Radway. *A History of the Book in America: Print in Motion.* Chapel Hill, NC., University of North Carolina Press, 2009.

Kendall, Joshua. "Melvil Dewey, Compulsive Innovator." *American Libraries Magazine,* March 24, 2014.

Knott, Cheryl. *Not Free, Not For All: Public Libraries in the Age of Jim Crow.* University of Massachusetts Press, 2015.

"Librarians of America." *New York Times,* September 13, 1890.

"Louisville Brilliantly Reviewed." *Chicago Defender,* December 7, 1912.

Malone, Cheryl Knott. "Louisville Free Public Library's Racially Segregated Branches, 1905–1935." *Register of the Kentucky Historical Society,* Vol. 93 (Spring 1995).

Nasaw, David. *Andrew Carnegie.* New York: Penquin, 2006.

"Novels of 1897: The Seven Best." *New York Times,* July 2, 1898.

Schlup, Leonard, and Stephen H. Paschen, editors. *Librarianship in Gilded Age America: An Anthology of Writing, 1868–e1901.* Jefferson, NC: McFarland, 2009.

"The Traveling Library." *New York Times,* May 3, 1896.

Van Slyck, Abigail A. *Free to All: Carnegie Libraries and American Culture, 1890–1920.* University of Chicago Press, 1995.

Wiegand, Wayne A. *Irrepressible Reformer: A Biography of Melvil Dewey.* American Library Association, 1996.

Wiegand, Wayne A. *Part of Our Lives: A People's History of the American Public Library.* Oxford University Press, 2015.

Wright, George C. *Life Behind a Veil: Blacks in Louisville, Kentucky, 1865–1930.* Baton Rouge, LA: LSU Press, 1985.

Wright, Lillian Taylor. "Thomas Fountain Blue: Pioneer Librarian, 1866–1935." Masters thesis, Atlanta University, 1955.

CHAPTER 10: WILLIAM MULHOLLAND

Barringer, Felicity. "The Water Fight that Inspired 'Chinatown.'" *New York Times,* April 25, 2012.

"Busy in Steel Mills." *New York Times,* August 6, 1911.

Complete Report on the Construction of the Los Angeles Aqueduct. Board of Public Service Commissioners, City of Los Angeles, 1916.

First Annual Report of the Chief Engineer of the LA Aqueduct. Board of Public Works, City of Los Angeles, 1907.

Fogelson, Robert M. *The Fragmented Metropolis: Los Angles, 1850–1930.* University of California Press, 1993.

Groff, Francis A. "Frank Wiggins, Glad Hand Artist." *Los Angeles Herald,* November 1, 1910.

Harrison, Scott. "Building the LA Aqueduct." *Los Angeles Times,* November 6, 2011.

Heinley, Burt. "Carrying Water Through a Desert: The Story of the Los Angeles Aqueduct." *National Geographic,* Vol. 21, No. 7 (July 1919).

Hoffman, Abraham. *Vision or Villainy: Origins of the Owens Valley–Los Angeles Water Controversy.* College Station, TX: TAMU Press, 1981.

Libecap, Gary. *Rescuing Water Markets: Lessons from the Owens Valley.* Property and Environment Research Center, www.perc.org., 2005.

Lippincott, J. B. *William Mulholland—Engineer, Pioneer, Raconteur.* American Society of Civil Engineers, 1941.

Matson, Robert William. *William Mulholland: A Forgotten Forefather.* Stockton, CA: University of the Pacific, 1976.

Mulholland, Catherine. *William Mulholland and the Rise of Los Angeles.* Berkeley, CA: University of California Press, 2000.

Nadeau, Remi. *The Water Seekers.* New York: Doubleday, 1950.

"On Occasions Like This, I Envy the Dead: The St. Francis Dam Disaster." Smithsonian Magazine. www.smithsonian.org, March 12, 2015

"Opening the Los Angeles Aqueduct." *Los Angeles Times,* November 1, 1913

"Owens River Water to Come Dashing Down Sparkling Cascade Wednesday While Many Thousands of Its Owners Applaud." *Los Angeles Times,* November 2, 1913.

Pritzker, Barry M. *Native American Encyclopedia: History, Culture and Peoples.* Oxford University Press, 2000.

Rathbun, Morris. "The Pioneer Community Advertiser." *Judicious Advertising,* Vol. 19, No. 12 (January 1922).

Reisner, Marc. *Cadillac Desert: The American West and Its Disappearing Water.* New York: Viking Penguin, 1986.

Sauder, Robert A. *The Lost Frontier: Water Diversion in the Growth and Destruction of Owens Valley Agriculture.* University of Arizona Press, 1994.

Shannon, John. "Fresh Meat for Bill Mulholland." *Heritage,* Winter-Spring 1991/92.

Standiford, Les. *Water to Angels: William Mulholland, His*

Monumental Aqueduct, and the Rise of Los Angeles. New York: HarperCollins, 2015.

"274 Perish, 700 Missing in Torrent Loosened by Bursting California Dam." *New York Times,* March 14, 1928.

Van Buren, Thad M. "Struggling with Class Relations at a Los Angeles Aqueduct Construction Camp." *Historical Archaeology* Vol. 36, No. 3.

Wehrey, Jane. *The Owens Valley.* Arcadia, 2013.

Willard, Charles D. *A History of the Chamber of Commerce of Los Angeles, California, 1888–1900.* Kingsley-Barnes and Neuner, 1899.

Zimmerman, Tom. *Paradise Promoted: The Booster Campaign that Created Los Angeles, 1870–1930.* Angel City Press, 2008.

CHAPTER 11: DR. CHARLIE MAYO

Adams, Samuel Hopkins. "Modern Surgery." *McClure's Magazine,* Vol. 24, No. 5 (March1905).

Bailey, Liberty Hyde. The Country Life Movement in the United States. New York: McMillan, 1915.

Clapesattle, Helen. *The Doctors Mayo.* Rochester, MN: Mayo Foundation, 1969.

Clapesattle, Helen. "Health and Medicine in Rochester, 1855–70." *Minnesota History* Vol. 20, No. 3 (September 1939).

Crane, Caroline B. *Report on Campaign to Awaken Public Interest in Sanitary and Sociologic Problems in Minnesota.* Volkszeitung, 1911.

Dobson, Mary. *The Story of Medicine: From Bloodletting to Biotechnology.* London: Quercus, 2013.

DuPuis, E. Melanie. *Nature's Perfect Food: How Milk Became America's Drink.* New York: New York University Press, 2002.

Goodsell, Jane. *The Mayo Brothers.* New York: Thomas Crowell, 1972.

Granger, Susan, and Scott Kelly. *Historic Context Study of Minnesota Farms, 1820–1960,* Vol. 1. Minnesota Department of Transportation, 2005.

Institute of Medicine. *The Future of Public Health.*, Washington D.C: National Academies Press, 1988.

Jordan, Philip D. *The People's Health: A History of Public Health in Minnesota.* Minnesota Historical Society, 1953.

Mayo, Dr. Charles. *The Physician and Public Health.* Unpublished paper, 1932.

Mayo Family Papers, Olmsted County Historical Society, Rochester, MN.

Nathan Straus Papers, New York Public Library.

Nelson, Clark W. *Mayo Roots: Profiling the Origins of the Mayo Clinic.* Rochester, MN: Mayo Foundation, 1990.

"Progressive Public Health." www.mnopedia.org

Regli, Ådolph C. *The Mayos: Pioneers in Medicine.* New York: Julian Messner, 1942.

Rosen, George. *A History of Public Health.* Baltimore, MD: Johns Hopkins University Press, 1993.

Rosenau, M. J. *The Milk Question.* New York: Houghton Mifflin, 1912.

CHAPTER 12: SENATOR JAMES MCMILLAN

Arbaugh, Thomas A. *John S. Newberry and James H. McMillan: Leaders of Industry and Commerce.* Tonnancour, Vol. 2. Grosse Pointe, MI: Grosse Pointe Historical Society, 1997.

Burnham, Daniel H. "White City and Capital City." *Century Magazine* Vol. 63, No. 4 (February 1902).

Century Magazine Editors. "Civic Improvement: A Phase of Patriotism." *Century Magazine,* Vol. 63,(March 1902).

Drutchas, Geoffrey G. "A Detroiter's Capital Design." *Michigan History,* (March/April 2002).

Drutchas, Geoffrey G. "Gray Eminence in a Gilded Age: The Forgotten Career of James McMillan." *Michigan Historical Review* Vol. 28, No. 2 (Fall 2002).

Heyda, Marie. "Senator James McMillan and the Flowering of the Spoils System." *Michigan History* Vol. 54, No. 3 (Fall 1970).

Hines, Thomas S. *The Imperial Mall: The City Beautiful Movement and the Washington Plan of 1901–02.* Washington, D.C.: Studies in the History of Art, National Gallery, 1991.

Joint Convention of Michigan Legislature in Honor of James McMillan on April 2, 1903. Washington D.C.: Library of Congress

Kohler, Sue, and Pamela Scott. *Designing the Nation's Capital.* U.S. Commission of Fine Arts, 2006.

The L'Enfant and McMillan Plans. U.S. Department of the Interior, National Park Service (n.d.).

Loomis, Bill. "Hazen Pingree: Quite Possibly Detroit's Finest Mayor." *Detroit News,* January 6, 2013.

McMillan, James. *Report to Accompany H.R. 429.* U.S. Senate, Report No.637, May 10, 1892.

Memorials for Senator James McMillan. U.S. Senate and House of Representatives, January 30, 1903. Washington D.C., Library of Congress

Ouroussoff, Nicolai. "Tradition and Change Battle on the Mall." *New York Times,* January 15, 2009.

Peterson, Jon A. *The Mall, the McMillan Plan, and the Origins of American City Planning.* The Mall in Washington 1791–1991, Washington D.C.: National Gallery of Art, 1991.

Peterson, Jon A. "The Nation's First Comprehensive City Plan: A Political Analysis of the McMillan Plan for Washington D.C. 1900–1902." *Journal of the American Planning Association,* Spring 1985.

Weller, Charles F. *Neglected Neighbors: Stories of Life in the Alleys, Tenements and Shanties of the National Capital.* John Winston, 1909.

Wilson, William H. *The City Beautiful Movement.* Johns Hopkins University Press, 1989.

Wilson, William H. "The Ideology, Aesthetics and Politics of the City Beautiful Movement" in *The Rise of Modern Urban Planning, 1880–1914,* edited by Anthony Sutcliffe. Mansell, 1980.

CHAPTER 13: MUNI ONE

Bionaz, Robert E. "Streetcars and the Politics of Class: Voters, the Union, Labor Party and Municipal Ownership in San Francisco, 1900–1913." Master's Thesis, San Francisco State University, 1997.

"'Boss' James Farley, King Strike Breaker." *New York Times,* September 11, 1904.

Brenner, Aaron, Benjamin Day, and Immanuel Ness. *The Encyclopedia of Strikes in American History.* Routledge, 2015.

Freeman, John. "Strap Hangers Crusade—The Streetcar Protest of 1907." San Francisco Bay Area Post Card Committee Newsletter, www.postcard.org, June 2007.

"James Farley, Strike-Breaker." *American Illustrated Magazine,* Clover Publishing, 1905.

"James Farley, The American Strike Breaker." *West Gippsland Gazette* (Canada), May 16, 1905.

Martin, Thomas C. "Bion Joseph Arnold." *Scientific American,* September 9, 1911.

McWilliams, Carey. *California: The Great Exception.* Berkeley, CA: University of California Press, 1949.

Perles, Anthony. *The People's Railway: History of the Municipal Railway of San Francisco.* Glendale, CA: Interurban Press, 1981.

"Risks His Life Gayly: Farley, the Strike Breaker, Does Not Seem to Know Fear." *New York Tribune,* March 12, 1905.

"2500 Strike Breakers For San Francisco." *New York Times,* August 29, 1906.

San Francisco Streetcar Strike. Walter P. Reuther Library, Wayne State University. www.reuther.wayne.edu

"Strikers Shot in San Francisco." *New York Times,* May 8, 1907.

Ute, Grant, Philip Hoffman, Cameron Beach, Robert Townley, and Walter Vielbaum. *San Francisco's Municipal Railway.* Charleston, SC: Arcadia, 2011.

Schrag, Zachary M. *Urban Mass Transit in the United States.* Economic History Association. www.eh.net

PHOTO CREDITS

p. 6 *Kate Barnard in Tecumseh.* Reprinted with permission from the Oklahoma Historical Society.

p. 15 Bain News Service, publisher. *Kate Barnard by Bain News Service / Bain News Service.* ca. 1910-1915. Reprinted from Bain News Service photograph collection, Library of Congress, Prints & Photographs Division, LC-B2- 2464-9, Washington, DC.

p. 20 *Denis J. Swenie, Chief of the Chicago Fire Department.* 1895. Reprinted from the *Chicago Eagle*, April 20, 1895, p. 2.

p. 26 Barnard, George N. *Among the Ruins in Chicago: No. 21. Bigelow Building, Front View.* 1871. Photograph in Oliver Barrett-Carl Sandburg papers, Newberry Library, mms_barrett_sandburg_bx_6_chicago_031, Chicago, Illinois.

p. 32 Col. George E. Waring, full-length portrait, seated, facing slightly left. ca. 1897. Photograph in the Library of Congress, Prints & Photographs Division, LC-USZ62-110609, Washington, DC, http://www.loc.gov pictures/item/94503130/

p. 40 Jacob A. (Jacob August) Riis (1849-1914). *Tammany Street cleaning before Waring's Days in front of 9 Varick Place.* Museum of the City of New York. 90.13.4.320

p. 48 *Frances Kellor, director of National Americanization Committee and head of the Women's Committee for the National Hughes Alliance to support the 1916 presidential candidate Charles E. Hughes.* 1916. Photograph in the New York World-Telegram and the Sun Newspaper Photograph Collection, Library of Congress, LC-DIG-ds-09944, Washington DC, http://www.loc.gov/pictures/item/2016651583/.

p. 64 *August Vollmer.* 1929. Photograph from the Library of Congress Prints and Photographs Division, LC-USZ62-69954. Washington, D.C. http://loc.gov/pictures/resource/cph.3b17374/.

p. 72 *Judge Ben B. Lindsey.* Photograph from the Library of Congress Prints and Photographs Division, LC-USZ62-36882. Washington, D.C. https://www.loc.gov/item/2005691422/

p. 82 *How the kids make their reports to the judge every Saturday morning.* ca. 1910-1915. From the Library of Congress Prints and Photographs Division, LC-USZ62-137720, Washington, D.C., http://hdl.loc.gov/loc.pnp/cph.3c37720.

p. 90 Bain News Service, publisher. *Julia C. Lathrop.* ca. 1910-1915. Photograph from Bain News Service photograph collection, Library of Congress, Prints & Photographs Division, LC-DIG-ggbain-14253, Washington, DC, http://www.loc.gov/pictures/resource/ggbain.14253//

p. 92 Bain News Service, publisher. *Katharine Davis,* ca. 1910-1915. Photograph from Bain News Service photograph collection, Library of Congress, Prints & Photographs Division, LC-DIG-ggbain-15012, Washington, DC, http://loc.gov/pictures/resource/ggbain.15012/.

p. 95 Coplin, Thomas, photographer. *Model of a New York workingman's home at the World's Columbian Exposition in Chicago, Illinois, 1893.* Photograph from the Chicago History Museum, ICHi-025095, https://images.chicagohistory.org/detail/en/4399/1/EN4399-new-york-workingmans-home-exhibit.htm.

p. 100 Bain News Service, publisher. *Com'r Kate Davis, Blackwell's Island,* ca. 1910-1915. Photograph from Bain News Service photograph collection, Library of Congress, Prints & Photographs Division, LC-DIG-ggbain-15224, Washington, DC, http://hdl.loc.gov/loc.pnp/ggbain.15224.

p. 104 Bain News Service, publisher. *Mrs. Ella Flagg Young.*
Photograph from the Bain News Service photograph
collection, Library of Congress, Prints & Photographs
Division, LOC-ggbain-1053-3, Washington, DC, http://hdl.
loc.gov/loc.pnp/ggbain.05035.

p. 120 *Melvil Dewey.* In *The Review of Reviews.* New York,
London, 1891.

p. 127 *1901 Library Class.* 1901. Photograph from the
Chautauqua Institution Archives, Olivers Archives
Center, 2015.08.13.s, Chautauqua, NY, http://
chautauqua.pastperfectonline.com/photo/3B1359DA-C3AC-
4C33-A211-935252844475.

p. 130 *Andrew Carnegie and His Favorite Magazine.* 1911.
Photograph from Library of Congress Prints and Photographs
Division, LC-DIG-ds-10676, Washington, D.C., http://hdl.
loc.gov/loc.pnp/ds.10676.

p. 133 Caufield, James and Frank W. Shook. Thomas Blue
and staff of Western Branch, Louisville Free Public Library,
Louisville, Kentucky, 1927. Photograph Record Number:
ULPA CS 079246, from the Caufield & Shook
Collection, reproduced with permission Photographic
Archives, University of Louisville, Louisville, Kentucky.

p. 136 Bledsoe, James W. *Portrait of William Mulholland with
a surveyor's scope on a tripod, ca.1908-1913.* Photograph
from California Historical Society Collection, 1860-1960,
USC Libraries Special Collections, CHS-14459, Los Angeles,
CA, http://digitallibrary.usc.edu/cdm/singleitem/collection/
p15799coll65/id/3543/rec/1.

p. 138 *Jawbone Canyon.* 1913. © City of Los Angeles
Department of Water and Power.

p. 148 *Mule power at aqueduct.* 1912. Reprinted by permission
from the Herald-Examiner Collection, Los Angeles Public

Library, Los Angeles, CA, http://jpg1.lapl.org/
pics50/00044530.jpg.

p. 156   *Charles Horace Mayo. Photograph by Hoseth.*
Undated. Wellcome Collection, CC BY 4.0. Accessed
September 15, 2018, https://wellcomecollection.org/works/
rwhzr68q?query=V0026827&page=1.

p. 167   *Franklin D. Roosevelt and the Mayo Brothers in Rochester,*
Minnesota. 1934. From the National Archives and Records
Administration, NLR-PHOCO-A-48223868(333A),
Washington, DC. https://catalog.archives.gov/id/195301

p. 172   Sen. James McMillan, half length portrait. ca. 1902.
Photo in Library of Congress Prints and Photographs
Division, Washington, D.C.

p. 181   *Composite of scenes of "the presidential party viewing the*
models" of Senator James McMillan's plan for rebuilding the city
of Washington, D.C.; Pres. Roosevelt with Sen. McMillan;
Secretaries John D. Long and James Wilson. 1902. Photo in
Library of Congress Prints and Photographs Division
Washington, D.C.

p. 188   *A unidentified man assists an injured strikebreaker in a*
tram during the San Francisco Street Car Strike, 1907. Courtesy
of the Edward Levinson Collection, Walter P. Reuther
Library, Archives of Labor and Urban Affairs, Wayne State
University.

INDEX

Please note the page numbers beginning with *n* indicate footnotes.